HOW TO GET THE GUY

DATING SECRETS FOR WOMEN TO STOP CHASING MEN, KEEP HIM INTERESTED, PREVENT BREAKUPS AND CONQUER THE DATING WORLD WHILE BUILDING YOUR SELF-CONFIDENCE

BROOKE CLARKE

CONTENTS

Introduction   5

1. Celebrating You!   9
2. The Art of Confidence – Work it!   17
3. Insecurity is an Ugly, Dangerous Thing –   25
   Don't be that Girl
4. Personality Traits Men Can't Resist   32
5. Tapping Into the Power of the Unconscious   45
   Mind
6. Wherever You Are, Be All There (Being   54
   Present)
7. Learning Man-Friendly Communication   63
8. Your Charmed Life   73
9. Making Him Feel Ultra-Important   80
10. Knowing What Puts a Man Off   90
11. Using Words to Your Advantage   100
12. Positively Positive Associations   106
13. Financial Independence is Hot!   112
14. Love Yourself Enough to Set Boundaries   120
15. Killing Dead-End Relationships – 6 Simple   125
    Rules
16. Be More Than the Woman He Fell In   130
    Love With
17. Let's Get Textual   136

Conclusion   143

There's a misconception floating around that you have to kiss a few toads before you find your prince. A kiss is a kiss, even if it's with a toad for a while, right? That would be a nice thought if only there were a good selection of toads to kiss in the first place. There are a lot of misters out there, but not all of them are Mr. Right. And if we have to get brutally honest about it, even Mr. Boring, Mr. Not Quite Right, Mr. Good on Paper, and Mr. Perfect for a Short-Term Fling are starting to get a little few-and-far-between.

All these other misters pale in comparison to Mr. Right, but it's nice to get their attention along the way, isn't it? Wouldn't it be nice to have your pick of guys instead of having to select from a small list of possibilities? Of course, it would be! Nobody wants to *settle* for the best of the pick instead of *the best*.

Heck, women as a species are tired of paddling in the shallow end of the dating world pool. We want what we want, but the guy we usually want seems to be dazzled by a Miss Not-So-

Right-For-Him! And attempts at getting the guy's attention can be futile – there's stiff competition out there, girls, let's be honest about that!

I get it. I've been there. I know you're tired of the rat race of dating, tired of going on dead-end dates and drinking your nights away, searching in vain for the type of guy that is truly worthy of your time. You're tired of meeting the perfect type of guy only to lose him to another girl or find out he's unavailable. You're tired of men who ghost you, or you ghost them because they're just not what you're looking for. And then, to top it all off, maybe you're starting to feel like a magnet for all those toads, or should I say Mr. Wrongs!

If you're truly ready to take the plunge and you're *sure* about what you want in a man, let's talk about the things that will attract the right one to you. Being the right kind of woman is what get's a man's attention, and that's what you're going to learn to become in the pages that follow.

In this book, you will learn effective methods to becoming the type of woman that doesn't just make a man take a second look (because we know it's not all about looks by now, okay!) but also can't stop thinking about you.

It's not about being someone you are not – let's be clear on that from the start.

It's about making positive life changes to bring about the best possible outcomes. It's about finding your true potential, the you that you deserve – and the you that he can't resist! You're about to learn a few simple secrets to becoming the type of woman that wows a man, not because she is overly suggestive, but because she's a quality woman. She's *the one*. You will be the one!

We are about to tap into your true potential. We will explore your insecurities and help you overcome them. You're going to feel more confident, and as you do, you're going to fall in love with yourself. Doing so will help you find that inner flirty, sexy, appealing woman that all men want to be with.

You will learn tactics to entice the man you've been looking for just by being your true self! You'll feel more attractive. You're going to know what to say, what to do and how to proceed when everything starts falling into place. This is no compromise – you are going to be able to be yourself but still be everything he's looking for in a woman.

Before we dive right in, let's talk about who I am and why you should take my dating advice in the first place. The first thing you need to know is that I'm a qualified relationship and communication counselor. But there's more than that to my story. I *got the guy*. I had my pick of absolutely any guy I wanted by following a basic strategy – and I am glad that I did.

I am a woman who has often left the party/bar and received glowering looks from other women who have wondered how I have got the attention of so many men in the room.

The truth is, I am no supermodel. I don't have the perfect body. I am not the prettiest girl around, and I don't work out regularly. Truth be told, I often choose a burger over a salad. The trick to earning the attention of men lies in other areas, and I would like to share a few pointers to help you enjoy the very same attention that I do! It's not a secret – it's a strategy.

Let's get down to working on finding you *your* Mr. Right.

The very first thing that you need to do is make sure that you are ready for real, life-changing love. There is absolutely no point in seeking out a meaningful relationship if you are still hanging onto feelings and emotions of the past. If you are ready, let's move on!

CELEBRATING YOU!

I'd like to start by talking about enhancing your best features. No, ladies. I am not saying you need to prink and preen or get plastic surgery. Believe it or not, what you see on television is not a true representation of what men like. Men like all kinds of women. What one man finds sexy, another may not. Keep in mind that you are somebody's type, and you are beautiful.

That said, it would be best if you put a bit of time and effort into yourself before you can truly get involved in a relationship or even start drawing attention to yourself.

Sure, you could get your hair done, paint your nails and shave your legs, but it's so much more than that. Men love to see a confident woman loving herself. If you're out with your girl-friends and a man is observing you, what is he going to see? Will he see that your legs are shaven, and your teeth have been whitened? Doubtful, unless you're pointing towards your legs and saying, "Look! No hairs!" Which, of course, I don't recom-mend at all!

Will he see a happy woman who stands up straight and enjoys herself? Or will he see a girl who shrinks into herself and doesn't seem to enjoy being out?

You have the power to tinker with what a man sees when he observes you, and I encourage you to pay special attention to that.

Your best attributes are:

- Physicality
- The ability to have a good time
- Being sure of who you are
- Your attitude to yourself and others
- Your personality
- Overall confidence

Having things in your life for *you see* what I mean when I say that it's not all about makeovers? Of course, taking care of yourself physically is important. The following sections focus on a few things you can do to enhance your best features and start celebrating yourself more.

PHYSICALITY

I did say it's not all about hair and nails, but ladies, we know that we feel good when we put in the time to pamper ourselves and look great. You don't have to be a supermodel to be the most attractive girl in the room. You just have to be a girl who feels good about herself and lets it show. Unfortunately, feeling good about ourselves becomes hard when we have tatty hair, unkempt nails, and unscrubbed skin, so spend a bit of time taking care of your body.

I strongly recommend you make a weekly ritual of the following. I make Sunday my pamper day.

- Facial scrubs
- Hair (I color every six weeks, and I do an intense moisturizing oil once a week)
- Shaving/waxing (this shouldn't be something you only do when you have a date coming up, ladies!)
- Eyebrow shaping (I color mine too)
- Nail maintenance (filing, painting, moisturizing)
- Foot soak, scrub and moisturize (nothing is worse than cracked heels)

In addition to these basic physical spoils, make sure you're looking after your body from the inside too. Getting enough sunshine is important, so have a bit of suntan when you can. I call vitamin D the happiness vitamin because it actually has depression-fighting properties.

Here are a few more ways to take care of yourself:

- Exercise (you don't have to run marathons, but you should get your heart rate up for 30 minutes at least 3 to 4 times a week)
- Drink at least 6 glasses of water per day (yup, ditch those sodas and cups of coffee)
- Make healthier food choices (sometimes choose a salad instead of fries)
- Get at least 7 hours of sleep per night (you will look and feel great!)
- Limit screen time (engage with the world around you – great for good mental health)
- Reduce your alcohol intake (if you're just sitting at

home watching Netflix, there's really no need for a glass of wine, ladies – give your body a break!)

HAVE A GOOD TIME

Sometimes I like to pretend I'm the star of my own movie – nothing over the top, just a little act to show I'm having fun, in case Mr. Right is watching. Men love a woman who knows how to have fun. Now, don't get me wrong. I am not suggesting that you make a spectacle of yourself by drinking too much, getting rowdy, or laughing too loudly while flipping your hair back and forth. Chances are, the *right* men are avoiding those types of behaviors. Instead, I am talking about being a woman who seems confident while smiling and engaging with those around her.

BE SURE OF WHO YOU ARE

Men are attracted to women who are sure of themselves. No matter what you've done with your hair, do it for you and rock it! Look at the musician *Pink*. She has a strong body and short hair. Some people would describe her as androgynous, and maybe that isn't a conventional beauty, but boy, does she rock who she is! That is what makes her all the more attractive. She doesn't care one bit what anyone thinks and she is sure of who she is.

Even if you have to fake-it-til-you-make-it, act like you're having a great time and feel good about yourself. There are actually theories out there that the more you tell yourself you're confident and having a good time, the more your brain buys into it. And before you know it, what you think is what you are. Think about that for a bit! It's true!

FEELING BEAUTIFUL

I am a big cheerleader for women who celebrate themselves. Men only really started to notice me when I learned how to do that. Men are not as interested in the perfect woman or sex-bomb as you think. They're keen on real girls. Down-to-earth girls who know who they are and don't pretend to be something else. Believe me when I say this, but what you might see as your flaws may be the one thing that turns a man on. Truly knowing who you are and being comfortable and confident in your own skin is hot.

Make yourself *feel* beautiful because when you feel beautiful, you look beautiful – I'm willing to put money on that! The question is, what makes you *feel* beautiful? Is it getting your hair and nails done? Shopping for clothing that suits your figure? Going on once-a-month salad and water cleanses? Hitting the gym every day or journaling? Figure this one out and start doing more of it.

CONFIDENCE, CONFIDENCE, CONFIDENCE

Men like confident women. You're probably wondering why I am saying this *again*, and it's because it's one of the most important aspects of getting the guy. In fact, there's an entire section in this book aimed at building confidence. The fact that men find confidence hot isn't news. Girly magazines have been punting this point to women for decades, and in most romance books we read, it's the girl who stands out from the crowd with her down-to-earth confidence that gets the stud's attention.

Men are attracted to confidence – it's true. Many psychological studies have proven this. Now, don't confuse confidence with being loud and obnoxious. They aren't the same thing. Being confident is all about being comfortable in your own skin and being able to hold your own. Being confident is being comfortable and at ease even when the loud and obnoxious girl at a party is stealing glances or throwing herself at *your* guy. It's knowing that you're quality – because you are. You can be yourself, even if you're shy, and still have confidence, by the way.

What does confidence look like?

- Smiling easily
- Laughing readily
- Making eye-contact
- Being open to conversation
- Having open body language
- Sharing in a group scenario
- Not letting the actions (or presence) of other women around you unsettle you

There's no need to throw yourself into the deep end. Instead, spend some time practicing being confident. Make eye contact, show interest, laugh easily, and don't withdraw into yourself. One thing that works for me is to turn the focus on others by asking them questions. Men and women love to talk about themselves, and being interested in whatever they have to say flips the focus and also makes them feel good. Being interested is also a great way to make a fantastic first impression.

ORCHESTRATE COMFORTABLE SETTINGS TO MEET MEN

Now, if you're anything like I was a few years ago and suffer from social anxiety or shyness, confidence and self-celebration might be a tall ask. One trick I have learned in that department is to avoid putting myself in awkward scenarios. You want to meet new guys, to possibly find the one, but going full-steam-ahead into a bar packed with male strangers is probably not the best way to go about it.

Instead, orchestrate your evenings. Go out with people you're already comfortable and confident around because you can feed off that energy and portray a secure and comfortable person – because you are! Another good trick is to try to meet new men through people you know. Heading to your best friend's barbecue is far more comfortable than going to a night-club, trying to find a man – just saying.

GET INTERESTED IN LIFE – HAVE SOMETHING TO TALK ABOUT

Men like women who have purpose and passions. It's true – you can totally take my word on this one. If all you do is wake up, go to work, and then go to bed early every day, there's not going to be much to you – sorry, girls! It's hard to think that you might be boring, isn't it? This isn't a stab at you – I just speak from experience. When I was first out there trying to figure out what men want, I discovered that I was a little boring.

I had no passions, hobbies, or interests, and I only really noticed when I met this gorgeous hunk of a male specimen at a party. I remember listening to him speak about his life and all the things that interested him, and when he turned the conversation on me and asked me what my "thing" was, I choked up. I didn't have a "thing." I had nothing to share with him, and through no fault of his, he found someone more interesting to talk with that night.

Hobbies aren't just great for conversational pieces but also provide an opportunity for you to meet other people who have the same interests as you. This goes a long way towards feeling comfortable and confident around other people – after all, you already have so much in common.

Another great way to find interests in life and pep up your conversational skills is to start paying attention to the world around you. It's easy to get into our patterns of eat, work, sleep, eat – rinse and repeat. But when a gorgeous man is standing in front of you looking for a glimmer of conversational hope, you better have something more to talk about than your regular teeth brushing and sleep cycles!

Paying attention to the world around you involves:

- Reading the newspaper
- Watching the news
- Catching up on sports (if you're not into sports, at least learn a bit about it)
- Talking to co-workers about what's happening in their lives
- Getting involved in after-work activities

The above pointers will help you to get started with enhancing your best features. Your best features can be enhanced with physical self-care, yes, but it also includes so much more. Enhance your best features by having a good time, being sure of yourself, adjusting your attitude, gaining confidence, and finding hobbies that give your life (and conversations) more meaning. Ready to move on to our confidence-building chapter? Turn the page!

THE ART OF CONFIDENCE – WORK IT!

Just like learning any new fitness routine, confidence isn't something you learn overnight. It takes work, especially if you're starting from a deficiency in that area like I was a few years ago! Believe me when I say this: confidence is a mindset you **can** enforce. Being confident does not mean perfection. We all have things we want to change about ourselves. It means being comfortable with who you are and being willing to put yourself out there to connect with others because you *believe* you have value.

Boosting your confidence is a bit of a workout, and the ten life hacks below will shift you from a not-so-confident girl to a hear-me-roar kind of confident woman.

TOP 10 CONFIDENCE BOOSTERS – GET TO WORK ON THEM NOW

GET YOUR SELF TALK UNDER CONTROL!

Speak kindly to yourself – if you're always putting yourself down internally, it can affect you in real life. Whenever I start feeling negative about myself or any situation, I turn it around to attract more positivity. Men can sniff out negative women with efficiency – they don't like it. Negativity is unattractive, even if it's towards yourself. You know women who always say to their men, "Gah! I have put on so much weight, and my hair is so ugly!" or similar on a regular basis?

Let me tell you a secret... men don't enjoy it. They don't like it. In fact, it makes them downright uncomfortable. But that's beside the point. You don't have the man to bore with negativity yet, so let's get your self-talk under control before he even makes an appearance in your life. You can't let self-doubt win, so how can you overcome it? Here's where the real work begins, ladies. I told you this process would take work, and it *will*. Below are a few pointers for turning your negative self-talk around.

MAKE A LIST OF YOUR STRENGTHS:

Take the time to do this. Maybe you're a good friend, or you paint well, or you're good at playing an instrument. Maybe you're intelligent about money, or you've learned a skill that is incredible. Put all of these things on the list and refer to them often. Heck, set reminders to pop up on your calendar every few days just to remind you how strong and valuable you are!

TURN YOUR INSECURITIES AROUND:

Whenever you catch yourself talking/thinking negatively about yourself, turn it around. Calling yourself horrible names is a terrible habit, and whatever you're saying to yourself will turn into beliefs you have about yourself. You need to make your self-talk positive and really start to celebrate *yourself.*

ONLY SAY THINGS TO YOURSELF THAT YOU'D BE COMFORTABLE SAYING TO SOMEONE ELSE:

Unless you're a really horrible person, you probably wouldn't call someone out to their face about being fat, unattractive, stupid, or similar. Why do you do it to yourself? You're a person too! Abuse is abuse, even if it's directed at yourself. Keep that in mind. When you're thinking and talking about yourself, stop and ask yourself, "Would I say this about someone else?" If not, stop and change the thought process. I keep a journal of all the negative things I think and feel about myself, and in a column next to these thoughts, I have recorded more positive thoughts to have about myself. I read it before bed every night, and it's really helped to change my self-talk.

DO NOT FOCUS ON SELF-DOUBT:

For years I watched my mother put herself down about her weight, but nothing ever changed. She believed these terrible things about herself, and it made her feel rotten. If you find yourself in this habit, do not focus on whatever it is that is bothering you. Focus on the positives, and when you're actually ready to make changes (more on that below), then you can shift your focus back to this trait and fix what is bugging you! Focus on your positive points. Make them paramount in your mind!

DO SOMETHING THAT SCARES YOU

Insecurity and self-doubt feed on fear. If you challenge yourself to do things that you fear, it stands to reason that self-doubt and insecurity will be starved right out of your life!

The more you do that scares you, the more confident you become. I'm not talking about cliff diving, but go after that dream job, start that business, go give that talk on your expertise, heck go sing at karaoke if that's what scares you. You will never know if you're capable of these amazing things unless you go after what scares you!

Maybe it's as simple as wearing the shirt you think you can't pull off. Pushing yourself shows you that perhaps it's not as scary as you thought. Next thing you know, people are complimenting you and you're saying to yourself "This is me in my gorgeous shirt, and I'm looking amazing!"

STOP COMPARING YOURSELF TO OTHERS

This point is the biggest culprit of self-esteem problems that can spark and fester – comparing yourself to others. Don't do it! If you're scrolling through social media and looking at some other woman's body and wishing that was you, just stop. Wishing you looked like someone else is not a healthy mindset, and you can quickly find yourself doubting your own strengths, comparing yourself to 16 filters and photoshopped models.

Subjecting yourself to these thoughts is not doing you any favors. Look at yourself in the mirror and celebrate your body for what it is. It's not just bodies either. If you're thinking things like "I should have a house by now, or I should have started my family by now," you need to remember that everybody is on their own path, and if you're focused on other's peoples' stories, you will undoubtedly miss out on your own. The chances are that someone else has scrolled past your social media at one point or another and wished they had some snippet of *your* life. We all have good things going for us, but those good things look different for everyone. You don't want to derail your journey because you were too busy focusing on everyone else.

BRUSH UP ON YOUR BODY LANGUAGE SKILLS

Remember to stand up straight and sit up straight. Don't cross your arms, as it makes you appear closed off. These are basic psychology tips; I'm sure you've heard them all before! Stop just hearing them and actually *listen*. What you do with your body can deliver all sorts of messages you don't want to send. If you're sitting at a bar with your arms crossed or staring intently at your mobile phone, chances are the hot guy eyeing you out is going to keep his distance because you look like you don't want to be bothered.

SLOW DOWN YOUR SPEAKING

Rattling off words quickly is something we see women doing all the time – we see it in movies and series and think it's the norm. In reality, it comes across as really anxious. Society has made women this way because we had to fight to be heard. Our sisters fought hard to get us the respect we deserve in the workplace and in society – and what you say matters! Speak slowly and enunciate your words because they are just as important as the next person's words and deserve their time in the spotlight too!

SHOW YOUR BODY SOME RESPECT – TAKE CARE OF IT

Take care of your body, not for anyone else but you! Taking care of your body is an act of self-love. Now I'm not saying run out and do 100 squats every chance you get, but if you're taking the time to get some exercise and feed your body properly, your body will thank you. Besides, if you're feeling good about yourself on the inside, you're going to shine on the outside.

Spoiler alert – men aren't attracted to perfect physiques; they're attracted to women who take care of themselves. It's a precursor for how you'll take care of them too. And before you raise an eyebrow, I am not suggesting you'll be serving him and pandering to his needs! You don't have to be subservient to take care of a man.

HYGIENE IS ALSO AN ACT OF SELF-LOVE AND CONFIDENCE

Take the time to clean and nourish your body with whatever products make you feel sexy and beautiful. You are sexy and beautiful, so enjoy a bath, a face mask, a hot shower. Whatever makes you happy when cleaning up should be a part of your routine. I personally love make-up too. I know it's not everyone's thing, but once I learned to do some natural-looking make-up, I felt amazing. You can find lots of tutorials online if you're new to make-up or feeling like you want to learn more - have fun with it and find your unique look.

ELIMINATE YOUR INNER NAG

Nobody likes a complainer! I have a general rule I live by. If I complain about things to other people, I have to be willing to take action and do something about what's bothering me. If it's not something I am willing to change, I won't bore other people with the details. If something is affecting your life/well-being, then change it.

Do you hate your roommate's dishes in the sink? Cool, move out, or have an adult discussion about what needs to change. Don't you like your job? Search for a new one. No situation is permanent. Fix whatever is bugging you. The victim mindset is not where it's at! I say this because I have seen many women surrounded by men in bars and pubs filter complaints into their conversations. I cringe for them.

It's not attractive girls! If life is terrible and you have insurmountable problems, you probably shouldn't be in a bar, and men don't like to be bogged down by lists of complaints, especially when they're still trying to figure out if you're their cup of tea or not. Unlike the fairytales we were told as kids, men don't want to feel like they have to save you the very moment they meet you. Keep it light – focus on the good in your life.

YOU HAVE TO LOVE YOURSELF ON THE INSIDE

The dating world has no place for imposters, so if you're pretending to love yourself and be confident, you're going to fail. Loving yourself on the inside is learning to embrace and accept all the little nuances that make you who you are. If you're struggling in this area and don't know how to get out of this, seek help. You can go through all of these tips, but if there's something deeper that needs to be addressed, they aren't going to help you. I saw a counselor for a few months before I started dating and got all that excess baggage out of the way – so there's really no shame in seeking help!

ADDRESS INSECURITIES HEAD-ON

I've always hated my hair because it's naturally curly. But once I learned how to do it properly, I realized the hair I was born with is absolutely beautiful, and I truly enjoy styling it now. I've embraced this thing that I cannot change about myself and made it into what I want. Do the research to improve whatever situation makes you feel insecure and empower yourself to change it. Tackling insecurities and turning them around is a wonderful thing you can do for yourself. It will develop the kind of confidence that turns heads.

I recommend working on these tips consistently to develop a more confident and assured version of yourself. It will really help you make great strides towards becoming the type of woman men can't resist.

If you're struggling with confidence and have a bout of insecurity and jealousy, too, the next section is especially for you! Let's turn to the next chapter to learn why insecurity and jealousy are ugly and how you can bust those bad guys right out of your life!

INSECURITY IS AN UGLY, DANGEROUS THING – DON'T BE THAT GIRL

Okay, it's natural to feel insecure now and then, but many women are so plagued with insecurity that they let it consume them. And if you're going to be consumed by anything, don't let it be *insecurity*. Let it be joy, happiness, and inner sunshine! Spoiler alert – those are the things men are attracted to.

Let me tell you something that a lot of women seem to overlook! Men don't like insecurity. It's really unattractive to them, so safeguard the object of your affections from this type of behavior. If you are feeling insecure, pick up the phone and call a friend – *friends* are the people who listen to insecure ramblings, not your man (or any man for that matter). Make a habit of avoidance when it comes to insecurity, and by that, I mean don't expose the men you are socializing with to it. It will merely make you look jealous and unattractive, even if that's the furthermost thing from what you're truly feeling.

Men who are looking for genuinely meaningful relationships are looking for someone who feels comfortable in their own skin and realizes that there is no point in comparing themselves to others. After all, you're beautiful, interesting, and attractive – and other people are allowed to be too. Below are a few helpful sections on how to banish insecure behavior from your life.

POSITIVE THINKING

The more positively you think about yourself, the more attractive you will come across, and that's what you want. Also, it's really attractive to see one woman straightening another woman's proverbial tiara than it is to see her trying to drag it off and beat her with it.

Think and believe that you are sexy, and you will look it. Think that you are easy-going and happy, and that's how you will appear. You don't have to be someone you aren't, but by banishing insecure behavior and reactions from your life, you will be developing new positive patterns in your life.

STOP RELATIONSHIP COMPARISONS

Once you are in a relationship, whether you are just beginning to date or you've been together for some time, there are other insecurities you may need to deal with.

Some people have a harder time overcoming insecurities once they begin dating someone. Relationship insecurity can destroy an otherwise great situation.

One of the best tips I can give you is never to compare your current relationship to your last one. Don't make your new person pay for the sins of the last person you dated. This can be especially difficult if your last guy was a cheater, but still – it really has nothing to do with new love prospects. This new person you are dating deserves the same level of trust you would expect from them. Let go of the past as it will not serve you moving forward. Some ways you can work on letting go:

Write a letter to your ex and really get it out. Then, burn it. There's no need to rehash old matters of the past. But getting your feelings down on paper will help you grow as a person.

Get a journal and write your feelings down. Do it daily until you just don't have the same feelings anymore. The trick with this one is to also have a "positive page" for each day in your journal. Here you can write new and developing positive thoughts and feelings. Eventually, these pages should overtake the sad pages about the past.

Hit the "block" button on social media and WhatsApp. This isn't because you hate your ex and don't want to run the risk of them messaging you. It's to stop you from doing that thing we all do – trolling. You don't need to keep updated with what's happening on your ex's pages or fire off messages to him when you've had one too many glasses of fizz. Blocking is safeguarding – do it and don't feel bad about it.

DON'T CONFUSE IMAGINATION WITH REALITY

We shouldn't read too much into everything. "Oh my goodness, he didn't text me back right away! Does he not like me anymore?" – this is a common downward spiral thinking pattern for us girls. Don't overthink everything. Having open communication from the start is the best way to combat such a mindset. Don't let your mind play crazy tricks on you because that's just what they are. Not everyone is the same, and you may find that your new prospect is just busy with *life*.

Not every man has his phone tethered to him all the time, and this leads me to my next point. Stop trying to mind read. You can't. Nobody can! So don't try. ASK. When an intimate text conversation turns steamy, and he disappears, ask him what happened. Try to keep it light. He may have fallen asleep!

Once you ask, don't keep asking. There is nothing more infuriating than, 'Are you sure everything is okay?' Especially if you're the type of person, who tends to ask this over and over. Everything will *not* be okay if you ask repeatedly. It isn't just annoying; it's an unlikeable quality to need so much reassurance. Don't be a pest (sorry girls, sometimes the truth is hard to hear). Trust him that everything is okay when he says it is. Step away from your mobile phone and *breathe*.

GIVE BREATHING ROOM & TAKE SOME TOO

Speaking of breathing, your relationship needs room to breathe. When it's new, sure, you're going to want to spend a lot of time together to nurture your fledgling relationship. That's normal, but it needs room to breathe. Don't smother it! Smothering your relationship is a breeding ground for trouble. Have your own life!

Remember we spoke about having hobbies and passions that help to develop conversation? Well, it also makes you a whole lot more balanced and attractive to the opposite sex. Go see your girlfriends, spend some time alone, play sports or whatever it is you like. He should be doing the same – time with friends and doing activities he enjoys. Don't be that couple with a joint

Facebook account to match your joined-at-the-hips vibe because this only screams of control and insecurity. It's not healthy, and eventually, one of you will need to cut things loose for a while. Trust me when I tell you not to be so available all the time. Men *love* the chase, and it makes you more appealing.

BE REALISTIC

Relationships aren't all fantastic rainbows and unicorns *all the time*. Like everyone else, you're walking on air in the beginning. It doesn't last. We aren't designed to be riddled with butterflies in our bellies and those high feelings you get when you first meet a hot guy. These feelings will ebb and flow, and you have got to go with the flow. Don't bail at the first time of trouble. If it's a lasting relationship you want, keep nurturing, and when things go sideways, be proactive and open to solving conflict together. If it's meant to be, things will work out.

DO NOT SNOOP

Even the most easy-going women on the planet are tempted to snoop at some point in their lives, so don't feel alone if you've ever found yourself trying to guess a man's social media password. But there's the thing: *don't*. Don't break into his Facebook, don't snoop in his apartment or phone. If you look hard enough, you will find things to misread, and then you're going to be acting weird. Act weird long enough, and you'll find yourself confronted, and it becomes a whole big thing where you have to admit you looked at something you shouldn't have. Just like that, trust is broken, and it's very hard to get it back. And I am not just talking about couples who are already together. When you're first starting to see a guy, chances are you will have access to his phone and possibly even his home. If you're caught being snoopy and insecure, chances are he won't keep that to himself. It will be hard to be the girl in the room everyone guy wants if they feel they have to step up their mobile phone security just to go on a date with you.

That said, go with your gut. Listen to your instincts. If something feels off, ask, don't snoop. And if the feeling persists, maybe it's a sign you don't trust him, in which case you should end it. Trust is super important in any relationship.

DON'T HANG ON TO THE WRONG VIBE

All relationships have vibes, but sometimes those vibes go stale. Maybe you met a guy at the local bar, and you've been sort of casually meeting for drinks with him and other friends ever since. This guy could be great on paper, but you're just not connecting – those butterflies you're supposed to have are absent, and you're now in a panic. Now what? Well, I'd say you shouldn't string him along – it's just not your vibe.

Relationships are supposed to feel good; it might be time to let go of the idea if it doesn't feel good. If you aren't having fun or communicating well, maybe he isn't the right guy for you. Know yourself enough to know what works and what doesn't. It's important to remember; nobody else is responsible for your happiness except you. Furthermore, you are not responsible for anyone else's happiness either. Do not twist yourself into a frenzy trying to please anyone but yourself. If you're *really* into the guy you met at the bar, but you can see he is more interested in another girl, don't be a contortionist trying to become the *type* of girl he might like. That ship has sailed, and no one is worth your efforts to be someone else – besides, it's not healthy to consider changing for the attention of someone else.

Managing your insecurities and knowing how to handle them can be a key component to becoming the type of happy, balanced, and attractive girl that *every* guy wants to be with.

PERSONALITY TRAITS MEN CAN'T RESIST

Masculine energy and feminine energy surprisingly have nothing to do with gender. We all have a little bit of each of these things in ourselves, and we swing back and forth to ignite these things when necessary. A woman in a leadership position will have masculine energy when she needs to command a room, but she can switch this to feminine energy when on a date. Knowing how to switch between the two is important. This probably sounds a little confusing right now, but by the end of this section, you may have a clearer understanding of what I'm talking about.

We all have our own personalities and characteristics, and you shouldn't change those by any means. What you can do, however, is develop a few additional traits that men find irresistible.

Here are the types of personality traits men love:

SEX APPEAL

Don't think you have to dress provocatively or let sugar ooze off your every word to have sex appeal because you don't! In fact, some of those things can be a real turn-off if you're too forward! Sex appeal is about being flirtatious in just the right way and making sure that you look good, but it's also about being relaxed, able to have a good time, and knowing that you are attractive.

You don't have to do anything extreme, but you do have to show off your best features. Pair your favorite outfits with a sassy smile or a flirtatious glance, and you will be on a winning path. Below are a few tips to help you on your way.

7 SEXY HABITS TO DRIVE HIM CRAZY:

- **The way you walk with a hip sway when you're feeling sexy.** Supermodels have mastered this walk, exaggerating it. This drives men wild, and it actually makes you feel sexier when you're doing it! Don't throw your body around dramatically trying to look ultra-sexy, but find a mirror and practice your walk – you may be surprised at how much more relaxed and at ease you look when you're walking consciously.
- **The way you eat.** Eating sensually and slowly and wrapping your lips around the food can appear sensual and is appealing to men. Let food light up your senses! You may feel ridiculous eating *sensually*. I know I did the first time I tried (thankfully, it was alone in my own kitchen), but give it a try. You're not the star of a porn movie, so don't go overboard, but

drag a little sensuality into your meal when on a date. Trust me, it works.

- **Whispering in his ear.** If you let your lips graze his ear, the hair on his neck will stand on end. This is one to tuck away for when you're getting closer to a man you are trying to date, but it's one that will work 30 years into marriage.

- **The way you sing to yourself.** Men love seeing you happy, and when you're singing to yourself while you're cooking or cleaning, men see this as you are happy and approachable. They love nothing more than seeing you in a good mood.

- **The way you dance.** Witnessing a woman's body moving to the music is attractive because it activates the feminine side – something men don't have and find alluring. Just like with the hip-sway-walk, this will make you feel sexier too.

- **The way you go for your dreams.** Men are attracted to ambitious women. This may come as surprising to you but gone are the days of being that helpless 1950s wife. Men like to see you going after your dreams because it challenges him to go after his! He sees you shine, and it permits him to shine too. A strong woman going after her goals is not intimidating to men. It's intimidating to boys, but men love seeing you excited about your dreams.

- **This last one is definitely one for when you're ready.** Men *love* when you're not-so-timid in bed. Saying stuff like, "I want you so bad," will drive him wild. Men want to be wanted, just like us. Have fun with this one!

PLAYFULNESS

Be prepared to play the fool or goof around. If you are too serious, the chances are that a guy won't feel like he can just relax and have fun with you – he will eventually move on to someone who can be a little more playful (sorry, again, this isn't great news!). The more playful you are, the more attractive you will come across. Being playful is about being able to have fun. Do a bit of teasing, laugh a lot, don't take offense when you are teased, and know-how to tease without being offensive. Being generally easy-going and fun is a great way to show your playfulness.

The playful feminine energy he craves will activate his masculine energy. Relaxing into a more natural way of being will make him crave you and chase you in an easy-going and fun way. It will also unlock that protective side of him – innately, he wants to protect you because you seem vulnerable at times.

This is not about changing yourself – it's about enhancing what's already there. Tap into your inner child and have fun with this. That ability to express yourself in a playful feminine way can be relaxing and fun. It provides a man with a softer world to exist in.

It works on men because the world is so masculine, and even your masculine energy has got you far, but that feminine side is fun for a man to snuggle up and nest with you. There's power in that, on both sides.

HERE ARE A FEW TIPS ON ENHANCING YOUR PLAYFUL SIDE:

- **Laugh.** Practice laughing if you have to. Put on a

funny show and pretend you have to record the laugh track for that show. It lowers stress and increases endorphins which are two of the positive side effects of practicing laughing. It's not weird at all, trust me – you won't *practice* forever. Men like to see you laugh because he feels good when he's around you, and it releases stress for both of you!

- **Make noises and do weird little dances.** I know this sounds weird. Create your own private playful language that is unique to the two of you. It's just cute. These cute little moments that become yours authentically are a bonding thing that works. He wants to have fun and create closeness with you, and this will keep him hooked.

- **Give him trivial questions or options.** Men get a little boost of dopamine when he gets something right. Try this: ask him, "What sounds more fun? Going to dinner and a movie, or hiking and then lunch at a brewery?" It will be the right answer no matter which one he picks, and he gets a little boost! Or ask him about whatever passion he has. Let him explain his opinion on music or whatever he is into, and he will enjoy being the expert for that amount of time. Men love it when women hang on their every word. You don't have to go over the top, but make it obvious that you love what he has to say.

- **Allow yourself to be a girl.** Enjoy your girly habits like taking a bath or collecting cute little trinkets that you like and let him see you get excited about it – he likes it. Men find this stuff endearing and sweet.

- **Enjoy the colors that make your inner child

happy. People who have playful energy are very alluring people. At heart, we all want to play like children sometimes!

- **Dressing for your inner girl.** If you're into it, add little playful pieces to your wardrobe. Do you like that blouse with little rainbows or hearts? Buy it! Enjoy whatever fun inner girl things appeal to you.
- **Pick up an old hobby you loved as a child.** Pick and arrange flowers, paint, work with clay, roller skate, whatever you enjoy.

All of these things fire up his masculine energy because he sees you as a little vulnerable and someone he wants to protect. Embrace your playful, feminine energy. Give yourself permission to tap into that inner girl and enjoy that power.

Of course, there is a time and place for everything. If you turn every encounter or conversation into a joke, a man will think that you won't be able to take things seriously when it's needed. So make a point of balancing playfulness with seriousness.

PLAY THE PART

Women with kind hearts, an open mind, and respect for others are highly desired. While some men might appreciate the "super-bitch," that's quite rare. Keep in mind that you want a man interested in being in a relationship, and that type of man is thinking about the kind of woman he will spend the rest of his life with.

Consider if he would be happy to take you home to meet the family, including his grandmother. Are you capable of presenting yourself to his colleagues and boss?

You don't have to be Mother Theresa, but you should think about how you come across. If you have been dancing on tables and telling crass jokes over shots for the last few years, you might want to consider making some lifestyle changes to support your new, positive outlook and mindset.

So, what does this look like? It's definitely in the way you dress. You could argue that it's 2021 and you'll wear what you want, but that won't change the fact!

That's all fine and good, but the truth is, you are judged on your appearance, and there is a time and place for every outfit. A night out at a nightclub might call for heels and a plunging neckline, but coffee on his lunch break might call for something a little more suitable. Imagine meeting his mom and dad for the first time in a short skirt and low-cut top. While it's great for a cocktail bar, it's not exactly appropriate for you to be flashing your man's father. His mother sure won't appreciate it either. You don't have to be someone you're not, but you should look at what respectable women wear these days and emulate that. Saving something to his imagination is a mental game that he will appreciate a lot more than if you dressed provocatively in front of his grandfather or, worse yet, his friends. Whether we like it or not, women get a bad reputation if they dress a certain way. Additionally, if you're dressed for the part and act the part, you've nailed it. You can dress sexy while toning it down a bit – I've learned to do that, and it works!

PRACTICE KINDNESS IN GIVING, RECEIVING AND BEHAVING

In discussing masculine and feminine energies, it's important to remember the anatomy of men and women, with women being the receivers and men being the givers. Kindly accepting what he has to offer with grace is a skill, and women find it difficult to learn at times, especially without feeling that they need to reciprocate.

In keeping with kindness, it's important to practice joyful receiving – the best way to increase feminine energy is to learn how to receive compliments and gifts with grace. Practice this: take a deep breath, smile, receive graciously. You're giving him the ability to give to you and ignite his masculine energy. When asked if he can buy you a drink or a coffee, a simple "that would be lovely, thank you" will do even if you're dying to say, "No thanks, I can pay for myself." The chances are that he assumes you *can* pay for yourself, but he *wants* to instead. Give him that! Watch his face as he gives to you. His face will light up as you have activated his masculine energy.

Kindness in front of and behind the backs of everyone you know reflects well on you, and the more you practice it, the more self-growth you will experience. Kindness towards other women is something that I would like to mention specifically. Let's face it, a woman who is ready to get into a deep and meaningful relationship doesn't tear other women down. Instead of making enemies of women you feel threatened by, show kindness, compassion, and friendship. Long gone are the days of ripping other women apart. If the roles were reversed and said woman was insecure towards you, what would you prefer? Her kindness towards you or her hatred?

Maturity means accepting *all* people around you and being able to show kindness.

MORE TRAITS THAT WILL AMPLIFY YOUR FEMININE ENERGY

There are lots of traits that men love, but the ones that make an impact include amplifying your feminine attributes that will unlock a deep desire in men.

FEMININE ENERGY WORK

Moving from in your head to in your body. Masculine energy is factual, cognitive thinking. Feminine energy is body and feeling energy. Masculine energy is straight-line energy, whereas feminine energy is circular energy. Simply put, masculine energy is about thinking and doing – coming up with solutions. Feminine energy is about feeling and moving. As women, we have had to tap into our masculine energy to get ahead in the corporate world and keep up with the whole "gender equality" thing. But the truth is that men are attracted to feminine energy. Now what?

You simply have to learn to tap into your feminine energy when you're around men in a social environment. If you don't use your feminine energy all that much, you need to do a bit of work to lure it out of you.

Tapping into your feminine energy can be as simple as practicing a few activities. Try some of these below.

- **Dance:** focus on moving your body to the music in a feminine way.
- **Get creative:** do pottery, painting, gardening – something that awakens your inner creativity.
- **Make pleasure your priority:** are there ways you can make everyday mundane things more

pleasurable? Work on that because it activates feminine energy.

- **Get physical and enjoy it:** do yoga, go for sensual massages, do things that are physically enjoyable.
- **Connect with other women:** a group of women together inspires feminine energy. Even if you just spend time with *one* other woman. Do it regularly!

Here are a few more in-depth tips on activating feminine energy that men can't resist:

FEEL YOURSELF

Wear clothes and fragrances that make you feel more feminine. Moving forward with self-improvement that highlights your feminine curves makes you feel good about yourself. Knowing you're smelling good and looking good as you lean in for a kiss and you can hear him smell your hair or your neck – you're radiating a feminine presence that is igniting his masculine energy. And it feels good to entice him this way!

TONE OF VOICE

I changed my tone of voice to a more feminine one, and men were attracted like bees to honey. I also started speaking more femininely, if that makes sense. I stopped talking like I was a man (swearing, guffawing, saying crass things) and started focusing on how I am different from a man in what I say and how I say it. It's a powerful tool to have, and you should definitely try it out.

ENTHUSIASM!

When it comes to enthusiasm, be just that! Enthusiastic. Men love a woman keen to try new things and get involved or participate without any awkwardness. If he says, "Hey, do you want to hop on my bike and go on a dirt trail this weekend?" try saying, "Hell, yes!" Instead of hesitating, asking about the facilities, or first checking who will be there.

FEEL SAFE WITH HIM

This can be a challenge, but it's a great way to be more feminine. Making yourself feel safer sounds like a strange tip but hear me out. Don't be guarded. Fight mode is masculine. There are two ways to make yourself feel safe: trust yourself to choose the right guy, speak up when something is off, or the relationship isn't going the direction you want. This feeling of safety and security allows you to relax, enjoy, and let your feminine energy come forward.

LAUGH!

Develop a sense of humor – find comedians you enjoy and learn a sense of humor if you don't already have one. Don't take yourself so seriously, and don't be sour or serious. It is impossible to flirt without laughter, and a woman who laughs is the woman in the room with all eyes on her (all men's eyes, to be clear).

GO WITH THE FLOW

Be easy-going. This doesn't mean you need to be a pushover. But if the restaurant you picked can't accommodate you, just pick something else together and don't sweat it!

OPINIONS - HAVE THEM!

Be proud of your thoughts, educate yourself, be interesting. If you are a boring person with no independent thoughts on current affairs or *anything*, it isn't going to last long. You don't have to know everything about everything, but it's always fun to have deeper discussions once the surface-level stuff is established.

INTELLIGENCE

If you find a guy that is intimidated by intelligence – scare him away! Men who are worth dating and partnering up with enjoy an intelligent woman. There is no need to be a know-it-all, as that is a definite turn-off, but being an intelligent human is an excellent quality!

INTEGRITY

Have great character – life isn't perfect, and he will notice how you react to challenging situations. Integrity and character are invaluable. If someone tells a racist joke in front of you, how do you react? If someone is being mean to another person in front of you, do you laugh along? Exclude yourself from the behavior, or punch the mean person in the jaw? I think it's safe to say that excluding yourself and possibly being kind to the downtrodden person is the way to go. These things can make or break a relationship for many people.

DEVELOP YOUR INDEPENDENCE

Make your life amazing, and you will attract many men. A woman on the phone with her mother and father six times a day is a red flag to men because codependency isn't attractive. Much the same, a woman who cannot go *anywhere* without her best friend is also a red flag. You should be completely responsible for your own life and decisions and make them wonderful for *you*. In later chapters, we'll discuss this further.

For now, let's page over to Section Five: *Tapping into the power of the unconscious mind.* This section will address how to tap into your unconscious mind to help you become the best, most attractive version of yourself.

TAPPING INTO THE POWER OF THE UNCONSCIOUS MIND

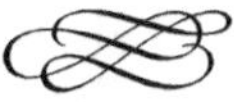

The subconscious part of the mind runs in the background, holding our memories, beliefs, experiences, and skills. It's a little part of the brain that keeps our human bodies and processes running automatically without us having to think about it. For example, our unconscious keeps us breathing. Stop and think about breathing, and suddenly it becomes conscious. At the same time, it starts to feel laborious. Why? Because now it's not an unconscious action, it's a conscious one. Interesting, right?

The conscious mind is the part of the mind that we use every day and are aware of. When someone is hypnotized, the conscious mind is put to sleep so that the unconscious mind can be spoken to and reprogrammed. With this understanding in the back of your mind, it makes sense that if we can train a certain behavior in the subconscious/unconscious mind, we will do those things automatically, just like we breathe or know how to walk without thinking about it.

This can be a powerful tool to ensuring that you are the type of woman that exudes confidence and the appealing nature that men are looking for, but more importantly, that leaves you feeling good about yourself. As you sleep at night, you can listen to hypnotic recordings, but that's not the only way. The more you think you are attractive, worthy, unique, beautiful, the stronger that message becomes in your subconscious. The more you think about it and believe it, the more it becomes a reality to your subconscious mind.

This part of the process can seem hard. How can you *think* of a new way of being in your subconscious mind? Well, here's something interesting. Studies have shown human brains cannot tell the difference between an imagined good memory and actual memory. You can read more on how the brain and memory/imagination work here: *https://www.ncbi.nlm.nih.gov/pmc/articles/PMC3815616/*

The thing is that both can leave you feeling great about yourself. Studies show that when someone imagines that they had a good time on the beach, it lit up the very same areas of the brain that actually having a good time on the beach with friends does. This means that your brain can accept and believe something if you imagine it to be true.

Believe that you have *a little secret*. And that little secret is that you are irresistible and attractive to men. I know, this sounds kind of corny, but stay with me.

The more you think and believe this, especially when you are in the company of men, the more your aura will reflect that. Trust me; men will be allured! You don't even have to say anything. Just think and believe it all the time, and it will show in your entire stance and appeal.

You can take control of your romantic destiny by rewiring your mind to be super, magnetically attractive. When you are feeling attractive, it will show through your confidence and facial expressions. Think of those women in commercials, smiling and exuding pure confidence, joy, and sensuality. When you are out, imagine yourself as the star of your own movie or TV show. Picture being the center of attention, with your face lit up and knowing that eyes are on you. It's a little mind trick that actually makes you feel more appealing to others, especially men. This is something I do at parties and at restaurants and bars with my friends. The number of times interested men approach me is phenomenal. It all comes down to that fancy little trick of the mind, believing that I am the most attractive woman in the room. In truth, I don't see myself as better than every other woman, but I do pretend that I am appealing to every man in the room!

GET THE RIGHT MINDSET

Many people believe that love is beyond their control. If you want a job, you will go out and look for the right job, and it's much the same with love. When looking for the *right* job, you will present yourself to potential employers with enthusiasm and your best foot forward. If you want a house, you will start looking for it. As you tour homes, you imagine yourself living there.

Yet, despite this effort in other areas, we do not take proactive steps to love and finding the right person. Instead, we expect them to show up on a white steed and magically complete us.

To find love, you must know a few things. In the first place, you're not looking for your other half because you're not a half. You don't need a partner to *complete* you.

It's important to think, "I am worthy. I am whole, I am amazing, and I'm going to find someone equally amazing. We're going to have an incredible life together." Make this your mantra. Write it down and read it to yourself *every* day. I am not kidding. This is the best way to get the message to your subconscious mind. Repetition. Not just repetition but a high level of repetition.

You have to believe that you are whole now and that you're looking for a partner. If you want to find love, there is only one thing you need to do. This isn't about going to the gym, eating right, changing your size, shape, or weight. That has nothing to do with it. It's all in your mind, and you have the power to change it! You are what you think you are. If you consistently think about how you're not good enough and everyone else is far better than you, that's the aura you will exude. And it's unattractive, by the way.

To find the most amazing love, all you must do is believe you are worth it and believe you are lovable.

HOW TO ACIEVE A MINDSET OF SELF-WORTH AND LOVABILITY

First of all, you were born knowing you are loved, which came through in your behavior. Babies tend to demand attention when they have a feeling: "Hey, it is 5:00 a.m, and I'm hungry and bored. It is time for a change. Let me wake up the whole house." And so starts the screaming and squealing.

As a baby, you weren't thinking, "Wow, my mother works nights. My father is exhausted."

Babies think, "I want it, and I'm worthy of it! Give it to me now!" Maybe not in those terms, but they sure know what they want, and the only way they know how to demand it is to cry out.

You might be wondering where I'm going with this. First of all, I don't suggest crying to get what you want. I do suggest acquiring the mindset of a baby, though. You need to stop worrying and wondering if you're loved or good enough to be loved, and just like a baby, *know it* and be ready and willing to receive all that you're entitled to and worthy of.

You can use the power of suggestion (on yourself) to make yourself believe that you are worthy of everything you want for yourself, and I don't want you to limit those beliefs to just love – apply this to all areas!

This means you're going to reactivate, re-manifest, and recreate something that was inside you once upon a time (when you were a baby). It may have been a long time since you felt as worthy of love, attention, and affection as a baby, but that makes no difference. It's still there.

You have to believe you are lovable just the way you are. Will you be more lovable when you eventually have thinner legs, a flatter stomach, nicer clothes, or when you have your hair done? Will you be more lovable when you have a nice household to bring someone home to or when you have a good job? You might want to ask if you should wait until you have achieved all of these things before dating. You might think that you'll be more worthy then.

I have one answer for you:

NO!

Don't wait until later because later never comes. You are perfect *right now*. Putting off love until you have better things or have become better in some way is what people do when they deny themselves, love. They wait. *I'm going to wait until I feel and look right. Let me wait. I will wait until I am perfect before looking for someone perfect.*

It is impossible to be perfect, ever, no matter how hard you try, because nature does not like that. There is no such thing as a perfect person. There are flaws in you just as there are flaws in me. Your best chance of happiness is to be flawed in a relationship with another flawed individual, having a flawed relationship. Sometimes the flaws are what make us and our connections all the more rewarding.

I'm flawed, and my lovely partner is flawed. Even our beautiful house is flawed. And I can tell you right now that every gorgeous guy you've struck up a conversation with who seems perfect is flawed too.

Don't get into the mindset of, "Oh, he's perfect," or "I'm perfect."

That's just not true. Do you know what you're setting yourself up for if you believe that? Disappointment, not perfection. Being paired with a perfect partner (if there was such a thing) would only make you feel lousy about yourself. Their flaws let you have flaws, which is a wonderful thing. It's comfortable – it's beautiful.

Decide today you are lovable, you are worthy of love, and consider why you love people.

Snippets from my life can illustrate this point nicely.

Years ago, I had a cat who was very special to me. He had a wonky ear, a lopsided grin, and his tail was missing. His flaws made me love him more.

My baby sister had a big toothless grin and little fat triple knees that I adored. As a child, I grabbed and squished them. In my mind, I did not say, "Oh, you need skinny legs," or "You'd be better with some teeth, and maybe some hair." We love babies with all their flaws, our pets, our children, and our friends.

Imagine how you love your friends and family members, including their flaws. This is how you should love yourself. This is the mindset you need to have.

ELIMINATE NEGATIVE THOUGHT PATTERNS

As women, we tend to develop negative self-thought patterns. Those are our go-to when we're feeling down or less than. We indulge in a session of negative thoughts, which only chips away at our subconscious. The more you tell yourself something about yourself, the more your subconscious brain will believe it.

When you know you're lovable, you won't have the negative thought patterns that most women tend to have. Some of these include:

"Am I good enough for him? Am I okay for him?"

"Is he too good for me?"

Switch this type of thinking around. Perhaps it would be a bit more productive if you thought,

"Hey, I'm awesome. "I'm great. I am lovable, and I am smart. My personality is kind, funny, and I'm good at everything I do. I am excited to learn more about this new guy."

You see, asking yourself, "Am I good enough for him?" is like placing yourself second. You're elevating him as better without even really knowing him, and you're diminishing yourself. Men aren't attracted to women who put themselves down. If you enter into a dating scenario with someone with the mindset that they're better than you, it's going to filter into your behavior, and that's unattractive.

However, when you decide, "I am lovable, and I'm going on a date," also say to yourself, "Gosh, I hope they're as lovable as I am."

SEND GOOD MANTRAS OUT INTO THE WORLD

You are lovable, and you are going to meet someone lovable. You're going to have a lovable relationship together. These are good daily mantras – start believing them.

Sending energy into the world that says you are lovable and worthy of love, is so much better than saying, "I hope he likes me; I hope he doesn't notice I'm 5 pounds heavier than when I saw him last. I hope he doesn't think my job is lame."

Don't do that to yourself. You're wonderful, and he is going to love and accept you or go his own way. Before a date, say some really incredible things to yourself about yourself, because you deserve to hear it and it will set the scene for a great date!

You are lovable.

You are worthy of love.

You are enough.

As long as you know you are worthy of love, you will find it.

Now that you're thinking about the unconscious mind and how to tap into it, let's move onto another important section that focuses on being present. Turn the page to Section Six: *Wherever You Are, Be All There.*

WHEREVER YOU ARE, BE ALL THERE
(BEING PRESENT)

Many of us spend too much time outside the present moment. We spend an uncomfortable amount of time ruminating about things that happened in the past or worry about the things to come. The latter goes hand in hand with fantasies about negative outcomes. This is not only time-consuming; it also evokes emotions that might cause unnecessary pain.

Ruminating can be a dangerous thing. It can make you take action based on bad experiences in the past. It can make you act in a certain way because you expect a negative outcome. It's far better to avoid the future and the past and live in the now. By being present, you forget about all the other things you are worrying about and direct your attention to having the best possible time right here and right now. When you meet men that you are interested in, be as present as possible.

As a woman who has many female friends, I have noticed a pattern in the women around me. I have heard it time and time again, "I really like this guy, but since blah-blah cheated on me,

I am suspicious every time his phone pings in his pocket when we're on a date."

Stories like this generally end in her gradually activating the cold shoulder during the date and going home in a huff without so much as a goodnight kiss. And all for nothing because Prince Charming sitting on the other side of the table, hasn't got the foggiest idea why she is acting so disinterested and saying snappy things on a third date.

So they go their separate ways, she has a hot shower and the type of sleep that's accented with tossing and turning, and he spends the night confused, wondering what the heck happened to the fun, interesting, and easy-going girl he first took out last week.

The next day she wakes up feeling silly for what she did. She has spent hours scrolling through their messages only to see that Prince Charming's approach is nothing like blah-blah ex from her past. So she reaches out and tries to create a new connection as if nothing happened last night. Except Prince Charming isn't an insecure guy and doesn't like drama and confusion, so he decides he isn't keen on another date. She may even get the "let's just be friends" text.

Alternatively, she is fueled by emotions and sends him pages of texts to try and explain why she acted so weird, which inevitably involves too much talk of her ex-boyfriend. While it's nice to know it's not him who is the problem, the new girl now looks a little unstable and drama-filled. It also appears that she still has a lot to deal with from her past relationship. His next step is, unfortunately, to excuse himself from the oh-so-new dating relationship politely.

Can you see where ruminating on the past and expecting a negative outcome can be dangerous?

WHAT TO DO INSTEAD OF RUMINATING

I've shared this tip with many women in the past, and I am excited to share it with you. Instead of getting caught up in your head when you're around men, focus on enjoying the moment *right now*.

Men love women who can relax and have fun in the current moment. If you are not naturally the life and soul of the party, don't worry because that's not every guy's cup of tea. Just be prepared to laugh along and participate in the conversation. If you like, you can arm yourself with some latest news and gossip from the world-wide-web before you go out. Maybe have a joke or two up your sleeve, just to ensure that you can bring an element of fun to a gathering.

You can do several simple things to get yourself out of the mental gymnastics in your head and start living in the moment.

MEDITATION AND BREATHWORK

Meditation and breathwork can help you learn to focus. This isn't a solution for when you're in the middle of a cocktail party, by the way – you'd probably look like you're in a coma or having a mild fit! It can be something you do in the bathroom or your car to calm your mind so that you aren't ruminating on the past or worrying about the future. Steady deep breathing while mentioning twenty things out loud to yourself in your immediate surroundings can help bring your mind and thoughts back to the present moment.

BECOME BODY FUNCTION AWARE

Another tactic is to feel what's going on inside your body. Most of our body processes are on autopilot, but listening to what your body is trying to communicate can be interesting. For example, think about how tight your muscles feel or consider the state of your digestive system. When you do this, you will discover that the inside of your body is a very lively place. You can focus on the now by keeping your mind on the liveliness.

ACTIVATE A SENSE OF TOUCH AWARENESS

You can also escape the plethora of negative thoughts in your mind by touching. You can do this in a variety of ways. One of them is simply sitting on a chair and observing how your buttocks touches the seat. I laughed when I first heard this one. I didn't really want to be thinking about my butt while out at a party but guess what? It works! Another method involves holding an object in your hands, such as a marble or a piece of food, and focusing on how it feels to your fingers. Focusing on the simple things can bring your mind out of a negative downward spiral. As soon as you feel that sense of relief from the negative thought pattern, smile, laugh, be present.

Even when I'm walking (I do that to ground myself), my thoughts constantly weave in and out of my mind. This has always gotten in the way of being present. To let the past go and to stop worrying about the future takes a lot of practice.

What can you do if you're at a party with him and suddenly you're in a downward spiral? You're starting to close up because your ex did some pretty terrible things to you, and something he said or did activated the negative thought pattern.

Now what? You can't run to the bathroom and do breathwork, and you don't want to ruin the evening.

Here's what you can do:

- Listen actively.
- Make eye contact.
- Position your body towards him and show that you aren't distracted by everything around you.
- Be grounded and real.
- Ask questions and genuinely listen to the answers without letting your mind wander.
- Show that you are interested in what he has to say and respond to it.

When a man feels that you are 100% present with him, in that conversation or moment, he will feel like he is the only man in the room – and that's a winning outcome! While men don't often talk about that kind of thing – they like feeling like that. If you want to get his attention, bring up something he says or reference it later on in the party again – this will show him that you were listening and present.

Let's move on to exploring a few more ways in which you can be more present when you're in the company of men.

PUT YOUR PHONE DOWN!

Due to social media and email increasingly blending into our real lives, we need to set clear boundaries on these digital tasks. Taking care of emails until 8 or 9 pm can indicate a problem, for example, if you finish work at 5 pm but still respond to emails at 11 pm. You should shut down your digital world at set times and do other things, including when you're around men. If you're out and about and want men to pay attention to you, being on your phone will create the opposite effect.

I would like to share quite a few pointers on this one because the instant gratification of constant connection via mobile devices has become a huge problem in society. It can be a relationship destroyer before the relationship has even started. *Here are a few tips to ensure that your mobile phone use doesn't deter the right men from approaching you.*

- **There is an expectation of answering and replying to messages and emails right away.** What I do is only check emails a couple of times a day which allows me to reply to all messages at one time. This lets others know that they are operating on your time, not the other way around. To this day, I haven't had anyone get angry at me for replying to a message or email the following day.
- **Social media is a big bad beast that eats up tons of time.** With all the validation that comes with likes and comments, it is easy to crave that dopamine high. It is possible to reduce your social media consumption (and you should!) in several different ways:
- **Don't feel compelled to share everything.** Like I said earlier, getting likes and comments gives you a dopamine rush, but too much of a good thing can be detrimental. Do not post on social media while you are out with friends. Focus on those around you and live in the moment. If you spend the entire time while out with men taking photos and posting to social media, you're not going to be as fun in real life

as you appear on social media – and that's not a good thing.

- **If you're addicted to social media and just can't help yourself.** If you hear the dingggg of a new email coming in, it's time to get serious about setting a time out for yourself. There are apps that let you control the amount of time spent on social media, or you can simply set a timer. I limit myself to 20 minutes a day. Once the timer goes off, I shut down those apps.

- **Disable notifications.** I assure you that FOMO, or Fear of Missing Out, will dissipate. It won't take long before you wonder why you turned on notifications, to begin with. You won't miss them at all! And if your phone isn't grabbing your attention every few minutes, the men in front of you will feel like they're having fun with a great girl who is willing to give them attention. Don't overlook how powerful giving a man your full attention can be.

OTHER WAYS TO BE MORE PRESENT IN THE COMPANY OF MEN

Of course, it's not all about ruminating on the past (or worrying about the future) and a mobile phone that can cause distraction. You may just be caught up in your head, lost the skill to be a good listener, or struggle to concentrate for long periods. I feel the same sometimes, and this is definitely an area of my life that needed a lot of work. For a long time, I would experience shallow connections because my mind was always somewhere else. Mindfulness is something that's hard to achieve.

In the presence of men, you don't want to be somewhere else. Trust me on that one. You want to be fully present, and you want them to notice that because it's a trait that men find irresistible.

Here are a few ways to do that:

- **Leave your agenda and expectations at the door.** Instead, listen and communicate with an open mind.
- **Make eye contact when talking with another person.** It's hard to be a million miles away when the person is looking into your eyes. Also, eye contact makes someone feel heard and connected (which is how you want men to feel when they talk with you).
- **Practice observation.** When men are around you, watch them. Observe how they behave when they are excited and having a good time. Of course, this doesn't draw attention to *you,* but it does make men notice that even if you're not the star of the conversation, you're there, and you're present.
- **Ask questions because this makes people feel special and heard.** It's a psychological fact that people love to talk about themselves, so go ahead and ask questions. Listen to the answers and ask more questions. This shows you are truly present and invested in the conversation. The guy will walk away feeling so good about the conversation you both had and will want more.
- **Remember what people have to say and use it later.** If you're attracted to a man you have just met at a friend's barbecue, remembering what he

has to say will prove to be a valuable tool. This may require you to actually listen and limit how much alcohol you consume, but it will be worth it. If he shares a funny story about his kid brother or something that happened at work and you bring it up in a conversation or text a while later, it will show you were truly invested and listening, and there is nothing more *present* than that. Men love this.

None of this is a tall order, and regardless of if you are dating someone or not, you will benefit from these habits. You can practice being present with friends, family, your children. Notice the difference in how they respond and how much more satisfied they feel with your interactions.

Now that you have some valuable tips on how to be more present in your interactions with men, let's move to Section Seven: *Learning Man-Friendly Communication*. This section will focus on how to speak *his* language, literally.

LEARNING MAN-FRIENDLY COMMUNICATION

You dream of sending your perfect man a witty message and banter going back and forth all day. However, you send him a message and get a simple, short reply. You take offense but should you really?

Learning how to communicate with a man is a great skill to have. One of the first snippets of advice I can share is that you can expect uninteresting answers if you ask broad questions. Instead, be a bit more direct in your messages to him if you're texting and make them interesting. As much as you want to receive an exciting message that gives you something to go on, so does he.

As a woman, you've probably received *those* texts before. You know, the text that goes something like "hey, what's up?" and then every message to follow is merely as boring as the last. I once had a guy text me, "Hey, what's up?" and then when I didn't answer, he sent the exact same message every day for a week. Embarrassing, to say the least – for him, that is!

Instead of saying, "Hey, how are you?" consider saying something a little more direct, like "Good morning! How was your evening? Did you get up to anything interesting?"

A bit on the bland side? I thought so too. One of the first texts I ever sent my current man went like this:

"Hey, you. I had a blast last night – thank you! This morning I did all the usual things I do, but while I was whipping up my PB&J sarmie for work (yes, my lunches really are *that* interesting), I thought of you and smiled. Which is a tad different from the normal get up, throw myself out of bed, and get to work by the skin of my teeth routine. So thanks for that!"

He still tells me it was one of the best messages he received. It wasn't hilarious, and it wasn't porn-star sexy, but it made him smile, it was slightly quirky, and he has never forgotten it.

Before you initiate a textual relationship with a guy that's caught your eye, think of ways you can be different from all the other girls sending him the "Hey, what's up?" kind of message.

Think about creating personal jokes between the two of you. Tell him a bit about your day, send him a joke, but be subtle and don't overdo it. If you are texting him first every morning, you are doing it wrong. The idea is to create interest without laying it all out there for him. If he knows that you are available every evening and only go to the gym once a week, all the mystery is gone. And trust me, men like a bit of mystery.

Keep things interesting. Tell him just enough to pique his interest. Send a cute selfie. Keep the details to a minimum and allow him enough time to reciprocate. You want to seem interested, but you don't want to seem overly available or desperate.

COMMUNICATING IN PERSON

If you are chatting to men in person, which is preferable, There's a right and wrong way to go about it. I have laid out a few tips for you below.

KEEP IT LIGHT

Yes, men do like to talk about deep issues and matters, but if you are heading out for a few drinks, try to be a bit more playful. Set his mind at ease and get to know the light-hearted side of him before you try to get too deep.

GIVE HIM THE LIMELIGHT

Remember, people love to talk about themselves. It's a basic human condition. Ask him questions about himself and engage with him. He will love being the center of attention and will genuinely feel like you have communicated on a deeper level if he walks away feeling like he truly entertained you. Communication is an art – I believe you can get it right.

POSITIVE TENSE TALKING

Create a new way of talking in the "positive tense". This is a great way to make a man associate your communications with good and positive emotions. Instead of saying something like "I don't like how we never go out alone – your friends are always there," you can say something like, "I adore spending time with your friends but do you think we can grab a quick drink alone before we meet up with them?" You see, you have spoken his friends up and requested alone time – that's enough to fire a man up.

You should try incorporating this way of speaking in all areas with men you like. By simply eliminating negative words or sentence structures, you can create a more positive approach. Think of this: "I don't like pizza, I want burgers for dinner" vs "I'd really like a juicy burger instead of pizza for dinner tonight" – note how the entire tone can seem changed, even though you are essentially saying the same thing. It's all about using the right words.

UNDERSTAND THE MALE BRAIN THOUGHT PATTERNS

Men, like women, want to feel secure in their relationships. Therefore, you should know how they think and how they communicate.

Men think in a straight line, using linear thinking, very black and white, cause and effect. If a man sees you feeling upset, he will look for a direct link to why you feel that way and try to find a solution. Men like it when you set a clear path like "I want to feel this way and here's how," with clear guidance and instructions on how he can make you feel good. It sounds too easy, doesn't it? But it's really that easy, ladies.

Know that men are fixers, and they reflexively want to fix everything. When you are upset about something and don't particularly want advice, tell him how he can support you by simply listening and being there to hold you. Specific instructions are extremely useful here as well. You can say something like, "I don't need a solution, but I really need to rant about Milly at work. Is that okay? I just need you to listen and pour the wine."

SET A CLEAR PATH FOR HIM

Men can confuse communication with blame or with something else. Have you ever been telling a guy a story, and he gets an entirely different message from you than what you intended? This can leave him feeling confused, stumped, and a little silly when he comments and provides advice, and your response is "huh?" You don't want the men around you feeling confused and silly; trust me on that one.

Set a clear path to help him out. I have found this communication technique vastly rewarding in my connections with men. Instead of steamrolling into a story and expecting them to catch on and run with it, I kind of spell it out for them to start with without being condescending.

If I am upset about my boss embarrassing me at work, I don't start by saying, "I got to work today, and then this happened, and that happened", and work my way up to the embarrassment. Instead, I start by saying, "My boss embarrassed me at work today in front of colleagues and clients!" And then, I go into more detail by telling the story.

It's much the same when you want to communicate to a man that you're upset about something – set a clear path for them to know they are not to blame. When you are upset, men are quick to blame themselves. Maybe it's that Mama Trauma instinct some men have if they were in trouble a lot as kids, but their knee-jerk reaction is to wonder what they did wrong. Others shut down or become defensive right away. So, if you're about to share some vulnerable feelings, men will want to shut down, becoming defensive, because they automatically think it's their fault. Make it clear to him before you spill your guts that your problem has nothing to do with him, and you just need to let it out!

KEEP IT SIMPLE

When there are a lot of moving parts in a story, men tend to lose interest, especially when they don't know the people involved. So, if you're sharing a story or frustration about work, know they might not follow it to the end unless you share a little bit of context.

Most men are not familiar with the social dynamics that exist between women. If you have a story to tell regarding the inner workings of relationships between you and your girlfriends, ground him first as to why this story is important to you. Having some context will help him connect to it. It helps if you describe each person a little bit. Despite all that, many men do not enjoy this type of gossip. It's best to avoid it altogether if possible.

BE ENCOURAGING BUT NOT PUSHY ABOUT EMOTIONAL TALK

When it comes to talking about emotions, men often feel like baby giraffes - wobbly and uncertain. When a man is talking about emotions, he is going to feel unsure. You should make him feel safe by encouraging him to share and remind him that you share a judgment-free zone.

DON'T OVER-EMPHASIZE TEXTING

Lastly, there's one technique that will bring a man closer to you. These days, it's so easy to fall into the trap of texting each other. Men don't love the digital space for meaningful connections. Texting most of the time is something we all do, and I'm not suggesting you phone him. Face-to-face communication is where it's at. It's where the two of you will become the closest, and because so much of communication is non-verbal, it's important that you invest the time spent face-to-face. If you're not firing texts back and forth all day, that's okay, as long as you're making time to see each other face to face. If you're not in a relationship, that may seem tricky, but a "Hey, want to meet up for a beer and a catchup?" message can remedy that problem with a guy you've got your eye on.

TIPS FOR TALKING TO MEN IN A LANGUAGE THEY UNDERSTAND

So, you're standing there in a group, and several attractive men are casting their attention between you and a handful of your friends. While it's thrilling, it can also seem overwhelming. How do you communicate in a feminine way in a language that men understand and are drawn to?

Here are a few tips to get you started:

- **Pepper your words with smiles.** There are many different kinds of smiles. Naughty smiles, having-a-good-time smiles, assuring smiles – you get the point. Making eye contact and smiling while talking can let one guy in the group know that you're sweet on *him*.
- **Be coy.** Don't get me wrong; you don't have to be shy or timid; you just have to pretend a little. Let him pull out a chair for you, offer you his jacket, and buy that drink for you – all the while looking vaguely shy and

appreciative. He will love it, and so will you. That's a winning combination.

- **Touch him.** Yup, if there's a guy at a bar or a party and you're thinking, "Wow, he is h-o-t!" don't be afraid to touch him. Now, ladies, butt grabbing and screaming, "Booyah, bring it to mama!" is not what I am talking about. The subtle art of touching is all about an arm touch here, a hand brush there. It delivers the message that you're open to touching him (and him touching you) without being overly raunchy about it (wink). It's a language men understand.

- **Be mischievous.** It's hard to tell why men understand this language best, but they do. Now, I am not suggesting that you rip the proverbial ring out of it and give your crush a hard time about everything because that will be a turn-off. But if you can tease him now and then, bump his shoulder or tell him wicked jokes quietly when no one else is listening, he will feel special.

- **Catch his eye.** When you're in a group of people, there are a lot of people to watch and make eye contact with. But at certain points throughout the conversation, sneak a glance at him and catch his eye. Men understand this as interest, and it will have the desired effect.

- **Never ever, ever, ever gossip or say mean things.** Men might not understand the dynamics between women, but most of them understand clearly that they don't enjoy gossip and nasty girls. They may joke and say things like "Oooh catfight" if you say something catty or mean, but don't misinterpret this as support or encouragement. A guy isn't taking the girl who down talks other people and has meanspirited things to say home to meet his parents. Remember that.

- **Find something in common.** It can be a belief system, friends, hobbies, or ideals. Once you know what you have in common, work it into the conversation. This doesn't just highlight that you have something in common but also makes it easy for both of you to have an easy conversation.

- **Play nicely with other women.** I have touched on this a few times in this book already, and it's worth mentioning again because it's really helped me in my quest to find Mr. Right. If you're talking to an interesting guy and another attractive woman approaches, do not play the mean girl role. Be kind, introduce yourself, be her ally. I say this because you never know if Mr. Right in front of you is *the* right one. And by being her friend, you come across far more attractive, stand to make a new friend, and might even meet new guys through her introductions. Women are not to be hated and feared – they're one of us – we should stick together!

- **Have something to talk about.** I said this in the first chapter, and I will say it again, you need to have something to say when talking to a group of men. They will undoubtedly bring up current events and sports while chatting with the other guys, and if you're sitting there looking lost, it's not going to bode well for you. So have an opinion, know the latest news and have a few funny jokes up your sleeve. This makes you more enjoyable to talk with – and that's a fact!

Now that you've got a good few tips to help you talk to men in a language they understand, let's move onto Section 8: Your Charmed Life, which focuses on creating the essence of a beautiful life (which is extremely attractive to men the way).

YOUR CHARMED LIFE

I cannot stress enough how important it is to create the essence of a beautiful life when trying to get the attention of men. This is what women often misunderstand. They think that creating the essence of a charmed or beautiful life (that's attractive) is about pretending – when it's not!

It's easy to pretend we are positive and happy people. Just look at social media. All the positive pictures and my-life-is-oh-so-wonderful posts illustrate this point perfectly. But the reality is, that's not the way to go about it. Remember that social media is a highlight reel of people's *best* moments – not all the moments. The reality is that not everyone is cultivating the perfect life behind closed doors, in private.

I have a message for you that will skyrocket your relationship success in the future: get real! Live in the moment instead of trying to capture the moment for a social media post. Instead of trying to make it *look like* your life is wonderful, work on making your life genuinely wonderful.

We all see it in movies: the perfect girl who works a full-time job has time to have a best friend, too many kids, and a few hobbies too. That's the perfect girl, we think. Well, you can be the perfect girl too.

Life isn't about going to work and coming home. If you have *no* hobbies or pastimes and your life isn't too interesting, you might find that others don't find you too interesting either. Before you can attract Mr. Right, you need to make sure that you are the type of person that's attractive and has a beautiful life to match. Those pictures you post on social media should be a true reflection of your actual life, not just a trumped-up photo of an average time you had with several filters applied to make it look better. Yes, ladies, we have all been there!

Create the type of life that will be fun to share with someone else. Here's how you can start working on doing that:

Make a list of hobbies or activities you can get involved in and go after them. Baking, sports, crafts, the list is endless. It's a great way to learn new skills and teamwork, plus you just might meet Mr. Right along the way. Revisit what I said about tapping into your inner child. What did she like to do? What's stopping you from roller skating or making crafts? Nothing!

GET INVOLVED IN SOMETHING

- **Join a fitness group.** Most towns and cities have a running or walking group and several sports for adults. It's a great way to meet more of your peers and get some exercise in at the same time.
- **Make time for friends.** Hopefully, you have a lovely group of friends, but if not, going after your interests (as above) will definitely find you some like-

minded people to share your downtime with. Get out there!

- **Travel!** Seeing different parts of the world, or even different parts of your country, can be so much fun and get you out of your comfort zone more often. So steer away from the all-inclusive resorts and get to know local culture!

- **Read!** Reading can open you up to so many worlds in fiction, but reading non-fiction, self-help books, and the news are also important to developing a well-rounded outlook on life. Dive into things you never thought you would read, like finance or something that will enhance your life and help you plan for your future.

- **Volunteer!** What are you interested in? Many places could use an extra set of hands: volunteer with the elderly, with children, with animals, even wildlife! Write down some of your interests and spend a few hours a week giving your time to those who need it most.

- **Arrange monthly events at your house, such as a book club or a cook-off!** How fun would it be to get the gang together and have a contest over who makes the best ribs or who dominates the nacho world? Your friends will love it and once you find Mr. Right, invite him too!

Having people to see and places to be is also a great way to appeal to a man. They love to chase something they deem valuable. The busier you are, the more interests and passions you have, and the more effort they have to put into seeing you, the more they will want you.

It's the chase! Men love the chase.

PURSUE YOUR GOALS

The 'perfect' woman will support and encourage a man in pursuing his own goals and dreams, but she will also have her own.

The mature woman has a vision for her future and pursues it with ferocity. A mature woman will be someone you can take on the world with. A mature woman will be able to handle anything. A partner in crime. A teammate in relationship and life. With that comes a feeling of security for him. You're reliable, mature, and consistent. Being a well-rounded, balanced woman is attractive. He will appreciate that you will jump in and help others, but that you will also attempt to beat him in poker, even if you've never played before. When you're getting to know each other, it's fun to introduce each other to the parts of your life that drive your passions or simply keep things lighthearted. Have something to show him about you – he will love it.

MAKE CONSISTENCY A PRIORITY

Speaking of keeping things lighthearted, we've talked a lot about being easy-going, going with the flow, but what about when things go sideways, or you don't feel your best? We all have bad days, but it's one thing to have a bad or a sad day and another thing altogether to have a tantrum if something isn't going your way. Part of being a mature woman with a handle on her life is being consistent.

Consistency is a valuable virtue because it lets your partner know that you are who you say you are. Consistency can be viewed as the opposite of volatility. If a man can never predict how a woman will act towards him on a specific day, if they are unpredictable and volatile - that gets old, no matter how beautiful she looks.

PRIORITIZE BEING ORGANIZED AND MOTIVATED

Staying organized and motivated is a habit that you can build, and these are key components to living a beautiful life. However, becoming more organized and motivated will take time.

Think of inspiration, motivation, and hard work in a circle. We can't all feel motivated all of the time. Something inspires us, and we get driven to start a fitness routine or a business. Then we need the motivation to work hard to achieve our goals, and then it takes hard work to make it happen (and keep happening). Being inspired can be as simple as having a good idea or seeing a friend go through a transformation.

Let's say you have been on a fitness kick for a few months, and then you decide you aren't going to hit the gym one day. That's fine. But then one day turns into two days, and next thing you know, a week has gone by, and you feel very uninspired and deflated. Instead of beating yourself up, as we tend to do, you need to find something that will inspire you again. Staying inspired can be just as much work as going to the gym itself. You may start to research fitness routines or fitness hacks. The information and images alone should be enough to inspire you. The same goes for all areas of your life that you're looking to improve, such as feisty career moves, saving money, and educating yourself.

Staying the course will be easier on some days than others, just handle it all with grace and do your best to keep going. Your life is beautiful because you made it that way!

PUT IN THE EFFORT

Be willing to put in the effort to create the essence of a beautiful life because it takes hard work to get there. If you think you can work at it once a month, you're wrong. Even if you are trying and failing at something, you're still miles ahead of people who aren't trying at all. It's like when someone starts training for a marathon. You're not going to run the whole 26 miles on the first day. Maybe you can run a minute and walk a minute for 3 miles. It's a start! You're lapping every single person who is still on their couch in their pajamas, and in a month, you will be lapping yourself.

Even when it's hard, put the effort in – men notice that kind of thing. And at the end of the day, relationships are all about giving. If you have what it takes to stick it out, you probably come across as the type of woman who has what it takes to work through the tough times in a relationship.

WHY REALITY IS BETTER THAN A LIE

You may question why anyone would want to put in so much effort to have a beautiful life when you can snap a picture and post it to social media while you're in your sleepwear on the couch. Everyone will *think* you have a beautiful life. Isn't that enough? Well, it's not really enough because when that hot guy you met at the bar last weekend checks out your Facebook profile and saw you doing all these amazing things and living your best life, he is going to expect it when he gets to know you better. When he realizes it's all a façade, the interest may dwindle, and you as an interesting and exciting person may lose your luster.

What's cool about creating the essence of a beautiful life is that you get to live it. If you make your home the place you want to return to at night, if you land that job you've always wanted, if you spend time doing the things you enjoy doing, you're going to be happier overall. You created that happiness, and it's all yours. Of course, finding a great guy to share it with will be a nice bonus, but if you don't find him in a hurry, there's no chance you will be desperate because you have so much going on – and what's going on in your life is of value.

Any man worth his salt will see how happy you are in the life you created and want to be a part of it. Being a woman, you want to radiate a special kind of power that men are drawn to. Mature women come with less drama and less baggage. Spoiler alert, mature women also see right through bullsh*t, so any man who is intimidated by her won't stick around long. No more dead-end dates for you!

It's not all about optics. Having that beautiful home, perfect job, and fantastic friends with your social media bursting with aesthetics is not everything. Be present in it. Enjoy it while you're waiting for Mr. Right to make an appearance.

Now that you're thinking about all the ways you can create a genuinely beautiful life for yourself that will add to your allure let's page over to Section 9: *Making Him Feel Ultra-Important.* This section will cover why men need to feel important and how you can go about making him feel it in a subtle way that will keep him coming back for more.

MAKING HIM FEEL ULTRA-IMPORTANT

Men won't tell you this, but they like to feel important in a woman's life. Now don't confuse making a man feel important with using a man. To make a man feel important, you need to call on him, but not excessively.

If he is good at something, as you will have discovered while chatting with him, you can use it as a way to ask for advice or a helping hand. Seeking advice from him doesn't mean you need to act helpless. Quite the opposite. Once he has helped you, praise him, and add quantifiers if applicable. There are several ways you can help men feel ultra-important in your company.

ASK FOR ADVICE/HELP

Perhaps you're at a friend's barbecue, and you notice an attractive guy who seems to be knowledgeable about stocks and bonds. You hear him telling someone about his success with certain stocks, and that's your "in." You can introduce yourself and say you couldn't help overhearing him mention some stocks

– ask him for advice. Thank him for his advice and stroke his ego a little by saying something like, "I have never met someone who has been able to simplify all of this for me quite like you have."

You don't need to be over the top; just be genuine and sweet about it. This type of positive reinforcement works very well when trying to establish a new relationship. When someone feels like you value what they have to say, they will be drawn to you – men and women alike.

Make the man you are interested in feel like he is winning a lot of the time. For example, if he buys you a drink or a meal, verbally reassure him that he has done well. You can do the same if he picks a good restaurant or maneuvers out of a potential accident while driving you. Making him feel like a king will do wonders for how he feels about you and attaches to you. Giggle a little more at his jokes, look to him for more conversation and be the most mischievous with him when you're in a group scenario – this will make any man feel important. More important than the others in the room, at least.

PRAISE HIM – USE POSITIVE REINFORCEMENT

Appreciating men doesn't always have to be task-related. Maybe you liked the way he handled a conflict situation, or something as simple as the way he spoke to a friend. Tell him! Let him know you respect him. Men love a little praise from women, even if they come across as humble.

Let's use this as an example. I once met a very attractive man who was involved in a lot of charity work. One of the tasks he works on is helping people in bad situations build their lives up again. He once told me a story of how he had helped a young girl beat her addiction to opioid drugs. He wasn't bragging, and I didn't think he was. When he finished his story, I said, "Wow, I am so impressed with the work you do. In fact, I am so proud of you. That's amazing." I kept this form of positive reinforcement up, which ultimately boosted his ego and made him feel ultra-important. We dated for several years after that.

TRY NOT TO REJECT HIM

Most women don't know this, but men can feel rejected in several ways. If he offers to buy you a drink and you say no, you can pay for yourself, that's rejection. If he offers to meet you at your place and walk to the restaurant for dinner, saying no may leave him feeling rejected. If he invites you to a weekend of camping, but you say it's not your thing and provide a counter arrangement, he may feel like his plans aren't good enough.

Reject him and his ideas enough, and you might as well say goodbye. There's a substantial difference between a woman playing hard to get and being difficult – remember that.

LET HIM RETAIN HIS INDEPENDENCE

You've met a great guy, and you're in the "hanging out" phase. You might find yourself overwhelmed with the desire to pop a few of your things into his house or take a selfie with his phone while you're out and save it as a screensaver. On the other hand, maybe you find yourself demanding to know what he is doing all the time or constantly check-in.

You might even try to make it obvious on social media that *something is happening* as a sign to other women. My best advice here is to stop, breathe, and take a step back.

Men want to feel good about their independence to preserve their sense of self. In fact, men tend to pull away from a relationship when they feel it is getting serious.

The way he tests you is almost subconscious. Whenever this happens in a relationship, you can feel good knowing you're progressing - if you pass the test!

The reason for this is that he feels like he is losing himself in the relationship. When he was single, and on his own, he did what he wanted! It can be scary, but you have to trust him, even if you've been burned in the past. It may be tempting to tighten your grip on him and never let him go when he pulls away like this, but this is where you need to play hard to get.

Men don't feel ultra-important when they feel controlled – this is the main message here.

What will really work for you is to be intermittently unavailable and allow a little mystery to remain. Not to play mind games, but that hard-to-get facade will draw a man back the majority of the time. Let him have some time alone as long as he hasn't given you any reason to mistrust him. Honestly, if he has, why are you still hanging around with him?

In addition, men need to spend some time with their buddies. You can give him the space he needs, guilt-free, and he will grow to love you even more. If you're just hanging out and know he is heading to the bar with his friends, don't go every time – give him space. Go hang with your girlfriends, and don't sweat it. The reunion once you've had time apart will be fun!

You must maintain your sense of independence as well. He is looking for confirmation that you will handle yourself on your own when he goes out. Don't be that girl that breaks down when he's away, and don't wait for him to call or text you once he's home or has finished his own thing. Just do your own thing!

To feel comfortable with you, he needs to be aware that you have a separate life from your relationship. You are responsible for your happiness. When he doesn't feel pressured to make you happy, there will be no stress in the relationship, and he's more likely to come back for more. He will feel important because you allow him to be him and don't have unrealistic expectations. Men *want* to commit to that type of woman.

"Absence makes the heart grow fonder," as the old saying goes.

HAVE A GOOD RELATIONSHIP WITH YOURSELF FIRST

It is crucial to have an honest, healthy relationship with oneself before having a successful relationship with anyone else. No matter how you look at it, this is a win-win situation. When you make a man feel super important, he can trust it because he sees that you are good to yourself too. It's not a façade.

It's desirable to be an independent woman. Take advantage of this brilliant opportunity to do things you enjoy when he's out doing guy things. He will recognize your happiness is independent of him, and he will appreciate knowing that you aren't a clinger! When you see him again, he'll enjoy hearing about all your adventures, and he'll be attracted to you on a deeper level than he knew before. Having something to talk about will be a good thing – I promise.

It is important to men that a woman knows her value. It is normal human behavior to seek validation from others, but you have to master your own validation from within. This can be a huge step for some women. It's normal to want to feel valued and worthwhile in a relationship, and it's definitely something we all seek. That said, an important part of a relationship is bringing it with you and having that sense of approval within yourself.

PASSING TESTS WITH MEN

I mentioned a test earlier on, and I would like to clarify that. For men, testing a woman they're interested in isn't an entirely conscious thing. So you can't really go and confront him about it – you will just get denial and confusion. Don't be that girl.

Here's how a test might look. You're hanging out with David, and he is all in. He wants to see you every minute of the day. He texts you, is funny, and has introduced you to his friends. You basically do everything together in the first two weeks, but suddenly in week three of "hanging out," he starts making plans with his friends and not you. He still sees you, but he is doing more of his stuff independently. What does this mean?

It doesn't mean he is losing interest, ladies. It means he is human and settling into things. It means he is testing you, but it also means he is hoping he is allowed to be him. Don't freak out. Let him enjoy his time out and about with his family and friends. Don't hang onto him, get demanding, or make accusations. And please, please, please don't cry or send desperate messages. This does not bode well – you will fail the test.

Be cool and calm within reason. I mean, if he is out getting smashed every night of the week and seems to be meeting other girls, that's a no-no.

Let him know that you have standards and aren't a doormat but don't have a grip so tight that he feels suffocated. A word of warning is that it could be a test to see how much he can get away with. He may not even realize he's doing it. The more you let him walk all over you, the less attractive you'll become to him, and the more he'll feel like you can't stand up for yourself. Likewise, if he observes that you have high standards for yourself by your words and actions, he will consider you to be a valuable person—he would like to spend his life with a woman like that.

Men like being challenged. Women and men are generally quite different in this respect. A woman wants her man to put her on a pedestal, profess his undying love for her, cherish her pure essence, and show that she is the only woman he will ever love. And if you demand this of men you're interested in, you can expect them to lose interest quickly.

Be careful; this isn't a jealousy thing. You need to believe that you are more than enough, very desirable and that he is privileged to have you. To keep your precious attention, he must also keep winning you over.

The effect of that mindset will be to lead him to continue to pursue you no matter what you say or do. Did you know that? This is exactly what he wants.

COMPLIMENT HIM WITH SINCERITY & SHOW YOUR INTEREST

When you compliment him, be sincere. If he's just arrived for a date, let him know how nice he looks. Just like us, men love to hear they look nice. Ask how his day was and listen to the answer. Ask a question or two. Next thing you know, he will be opening up to you about whatever is going on in his life, which brings me to my next point.

SUPPORT HIM

If he's making some major decisions at work or in life, he may need an ear to listen and a little support to encourage him in the right direction. If he's going after a big client or a promotion, offer to role-play the interviews or presentation with him and see what he says. Now, if he truly doesn't want help, that's okay. Don't take it personally. Ask about the promotion, the project, or the big deal that's just come through – he will be impressed you're interested and that you remembered.

GIVE HIM SPACE

I have already touched on this and would like to touch on it again because it's really that important. I wouldn't have experienced my success with men if I didn't have this little space-giving trick up my sleeve. Nobody enjoys a sense of suffocation in a relationship, least of all men. If he's working and has a big project due, do not whine that he isn't spending enough time with you. He is going after his goals. Instead of crowding him, rather find something else to do. Let him know you are there for him as soon as he needs you.

MAKING HIM FEEL SPECIAL & IMPORTANT THE FUN WAY!

That's enough of the heavy stuff. You can do a few fun things that may just make him feel that extra special tingle when he sees you. Some of these things can be a little cheesy, but I assure you, most men will appreciate them!

Here are some of my top tips:

- **Keep his favorite beer in your fridge.** How sweet would it be to come to see the woman he likes, and voila! She has stocked your favorite beer. I'm not even a guy, and I would appreciate this! If you're not at the stage where you're doing home visits, make a point of finding out what his favorite drink is and have it waiting for him when he arrives.

- **Long hugs are the best.** When you see him, hug him hello! Everyone could use a hug, and a long lingering one is just the *chef's kiss*! Besides, it feels good for you too and costs nothing. According to science (and you can't argue with science), a hug for 20 seconds or longer inspires the release of oxytocin. This hormone helps humans bond and connect, so hug him a little longer when he meets you – you will deliver the right message, make him feel important, and serve him up a delightful dose of oxytocin.

- **Touch him.** When you're curled up watching a movie, scratch the back of his head, snuggle in, just being affectionate can be so sweet. Give him a back scratch if you're so inclined. Touching is a powerful way to connect, and it doesn't necessarily have to be sexual.

- **Learn how to cook his favorite meal.** I know; it's a cheesy one! But it's a thoughtful gesture to learn what someone's favorite meal is and then put the effort in to make it. It might lead to the two of you cooking together in the kitchen, and that is romantic! You can use this to get a little alone time with a guy you like and ease the awkwardness of a one-on-one meetup because you will have an activity to do together. If you hear your crush saying he loves Bolognese, hey presto, use it to say something like,

"Why don't you come over on Friday and see if we can make it together?" He will feel super important that you want to treat him to his favorite and will love the idea of spending some time with you.

- **Spoil him.** If you have just met a guy, you probably don't want to send him a gift, but if you have been having drinks and hanging out a few times, think of a way to spoil him. Listen to him intently when he speaks because you might pick up on interesting snippets that make for great personalized gifts. Perhaps he lets slip who his favorite author is – you can buy him a book. Get creative with this one.

Master these things, and it won't take him long to recognize you are the prize worth winning again and again.

Now that you have an idea of what makes men feel important let's move onto Section 10: *The Fastest Ways to Turn a Man Off*. The following chapter will address knowing what puts men off and how to avoid that behavior entirely.

KNOWING WHAT PUTS A MAN OFF

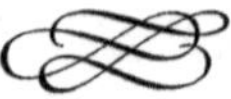

Here's the cold hard truth; certain qualities turn men off. And if you're dealing with a quality, genuine guy, certain things will turn him off faster than you can "fizzle out." In the same way that we run from red flags when seeking a good man, they do the same when looking for a good woman. I've put together a list of not-so-great traits, habits, and behaviors that you should consider striking right out of your life if you want to find, attract, and keep a good man. You don't want to be *that* girl, do you?

BEING A DEBBIE DRAMA

An emotionally unstable woman who cannot act appropriately is a big turn-off, especially when the relationship is still young. Drama creates stress, and if he is feeling stressed in your presence, he will not want to stick around for long. Now the drama you create doesn't even have to be directed at him to be fully noticed by him. He will notice how you handle things that go wrong. He will notice if you make a mountain out of a molehill or bring sensibility and peace to a standstill. Let's say you return to your car after a date, and you see someone has hit your headlight and not left a note. Of course, you're going to be annoyed by a hit-and-run, but nobody has been hurt. If you freak out and act super angry about it to the point that he feels he needs to calm you down, he's not going to have a great impression of you.

Alternately, if you calmly check over the rest of the car, ensuring it's safe to drive, take a few pictures, and send them off to your insurance company and then drive home, he's going to think, "Hey, this girl handles herself well." It's the same if you see him freak out over minor things. You're going to wonder what life would be like with him if he's a hothead.

It's similar when it comes to how you handle other people. For example, has another girl inadvertently made eyes at your guy in a bar? What do you do? Shrug it off and focus on having a good time, or do you storm over to her and get all "mean girl" and up in her face? I think you know what the right answer is here.

How dramatic you get with *him* is also important. Imagine being a guy who goes out with his friends one night, and the woman he just started dating is blowing up his phone, begging him to hang out. She's being dramatic and telling him he needs to come over immediately. She's texted every minute or so or called incessantly. He would probably switch his phone off and carry on with his night. Stay calm and easy-going. Save the drama for your mama!

INSECURITY

Insecurity is a relationship killer. It has the ability to suck the joy out of the moment and bring the flow of an otherwise beautiful relationship to a grinding halt.

Ladies, here's the truth: being secure in yourself is hot! So don't get all weird around him if you have a day where you don't feel as cute as you'd like to. And please, ladies, save the "does my butt look fat in this" speech for your girlfriends! Don't ever down-talk your own body and put him on the spot. "My legs are too fat", and "My belly is bulging", and "My neck is too short" are all passion killers – no man wants to hear you saying these things. Not only does he *not* know how to respond, but it's offputting and makes him feel like he has to put the effort into pepping you up constantly. Besides, if you do feel these are your worst areas, the last thing you should do is draw his attention to them, right?

Men like women who are comfortable with who they are. If you feel overweight and uncomfortable, set up a workout schedule and don't drag him into the harmful world of self-body-shaming. Men don't know how to handle it, and while they may provide reassurance at first, it gets old and unattractive very quickly.

JEALOUSY

If you question a man's every move or show open jealousy towards other women in the group or immediate vicinity, chances are he's already planning his escape from you. When you first meet men you like, you would probably never let them know if you feel jealous and insecure. The best thing to do is to keep this up even if you've hung out a few times.

I will share a gold nugget with you, and it's something that has helped my dating life (and now relationship) flourish: *feeling something doesn't mean that you have to act on it*. I have a little saying I tell myself when I feel insecure, "just sit with the feeling." Let it pass. It *will* pass, and the guy you're sweet on will think you're the coolest girl around – that's a fact!

Jealousy is an ugly quality, and it's best to keep the green-eyed monster under control if you don't want to chase the man you like into other women's arms. Don't freak out about his friendships with other girls. Believe it or not, the man you like probably had female friends before you, and they will be the first to tell him that you are "nuts" if you express a poor opinion about his friends. Play it cool. Any negative talk about his friends-who-happen-to-be-girls ends up making you look terrible. It also deems the other woman a worthy competitor. After all, if you're so insecure, there must be a reason, right? Perhaps she's a catch after all. You don't want to go down that road, ladies. The less interest you show in his interactions with other women on social media and mobile phones, the more secure you will seem. Even if you're feeling insecure on the inside, get over it. If he is genuinely interested in you, those friendships will be just that. There's no reason for you to interject.

If it's the early days of dating this guy, he has every right to be speaking to other women. Playing the field is healthy, and you can do this too. Neither one of you have to share anything about your other dates, and once you have that conversation to become exclusive, then all other relationships need to end.

STAGE FIVE CLINGERS

I have a friend, Matt, who was just getting back into the dating realm last year. I distinctly remember one particular catchup session with Matt where he told me about some of the dates he had experienced. We were sitting at a busy bar enjoying a beer when suddenly Matt dived dramatically under the table and hissed, "Shhh!" Of course, I found this highly amusing, but I had no idea what was going on. Apparently, a girl he had gone on a few dates with had just entered the bar, and she was what he called a "stage five clinger." As it turns out, after two drinks dates, she started to bombard him with messages, wanted to go everywhere with him, and basically gave him no breathing room. He had spent a week avoiding her, but of course, she knew his favorite bar, and in true stage five clinger style, she had arrived to scout around for him. Yikes. None of us wants to be that girl. If you are that girl, stop *right now!*

Men want to feel needed and wanted, but you need to find a careful balance between focusing on your own life and paying him attention. If you constantly text and ask about his every move or expect to keep up hours of banter via text or social media throughout the day, the chances are that he will feel smothered. Men like a cool girl who can handle herself. Men love women who have their own lives and their own interests. It creates curiosity and intrigue. If you are sending a man minute-by-minute updates on your daily activities, please don't. Leave room for a little mystery and intrigue.

PLANNING YOUR WEDDING AND BABY NAMES

Men do want to have meaningful relationships and a healthy future with someone, but if they start to like someone and that someone starts talking about marriage and babies and meeting the parents, they feel like it's too much too soon and run a mile (even two!). Even if you see this man as your future husband, allow him to take things at his own pace. Remember, while men aren't averse to commitment, they don't want to be forced into it or feel lured. Just be natural and be yourself. If it's meant to be, you will both know - there's no need for excessive planning.

Much the same, calling him "Boo-boo" and "Schnoekems" when you're just "hanging out" is an absolute no-no. In fact, it's probably a no-no all the time, but we all know that these little names can sneak into a relationship. So rather save the baby names for after he has fallen desperately in love with you – the chances are that they won't send him running then, but right now, play it cool and use your grown-up words!

A WORD ABOUT FEELINGS

It comes as absolutely no surprise that men are complete scaredy-cats regarding their feelings and emotions. Many women believe that men are void of emotions, but they aren't. The thing is, men, feel intensely, but they are not always willing to show their feelings.

Talking about feelings has its time and place. Don't spend time trying to lure a man into telling you how he feels about you because that's more about you and your ego than him. If you're needy in that way, pick up a romance novel and devour its contents. Men just don't go around telling women what they think and feel about them all the time, and that's okay.

TRAUMA

Don't talk about past bad experiences and traumas when getting to know a guy or socializing in a group of men. I know that sounds a bit harsh, but those types of things are probably very sensitive topics for you, and sharing them with men can paint you as someone looking for attention, even if you believe that isn't the case. These intimate topics need to be shared with people who love you or with a therapist. Sharing them prematurely in a relationship does not create a bond; it makes you look needy.

Men will feel overwhelmed knowing that you went through such terrifying experiences, but they don't really know how to respond. So keep the scary, sad, intense stories for later on, when you're in the relationship, and it's appropriate to share on a deeper level. The beginning stages are about fun and bonding in a much lighter manner.

THE DREADED EX-BOYFRIENDS

Don't badmouth your exes. This one is rather self-explanatory. Sometimes things go wrong in a relationship and don't work out. Men you're trying to attract need to know that you're not the type of girl who destroys a guy's reputation when things don't go as planned. If he can see that you handle negative experiences with class and style, you will immediately be more attractive to him. In fact, if you can help it, just never talk about your exes. Save those conversations for your girlfriends.

NEGATIVITY

If you have a pattern of negativity, always finding what's wrong in any situation, I'm sorry, but you're not someone anyone will enjoy being around. If a guy suggests going to a concert and you're whining on, "it's going to be too crowded," "it's supposed to rain," or "I don't want to spend that kind of money," you are Little Miss Bringdown, and eventually he is going to stop inviting you to things or start avoiding you altogether.

The same applies if you seem to find fault with everyone around you. If you arrive at a dinner and drinks session and lay down a diatribe about how awful your co-workers are, or how your friends are disappointing you in 87 ways, he's going to see you talking poorly about other people, and in his mind, he will be thinking, "she might like me right now but when she's upset with me..."

Cut it out, Captain Buzzkill!

BEING LATE

The most limited commodity we all have is time. Now, if you've arranged a date with a guy for 7 p.m. and he shows up to pick you up or is meeting you at a café, he's expecting you to be there by 7 p.m. If you don't show up until 7:30 p.m. or later, or you make him wait on your couch while you get ready for an hour, that's a huge turn-off. He's not only going to feel disrespected, but subconsciously he's going to think that you think you're more important than him. It's not cute or cool to be habitually late. It's rude. Do you want to be perceived as rude? How would you feel if he was the one who was always late?

UNSOLICITED ADVICE

Women are hardwired to make everything better around them. Whether it be your living space, your work, or the entire world, we are always looking to make things better! This is a lovely quality about women, but some of us need to pump the brakes on this.

If your guy is talking about a problem in his life, just listen. If you chime in with 18 solutions on fixing his relationship with his boss, it communicates that you don't trust him to make his own decisions. Monitor the amount of advice you're giving the men around you. Even small tidbits of advice can be off-putting: where to park, how to drive, what to wear. Now, if he's asking for suggestions, go for it! If he isn't, let him do things however he wishes and support whatever he chooses for himself.

A couple of friends of mine got into quite the conflict once they had their first baby. Every time the husband would go to care for the baby – hold him, change his diaper, feed him, the wife would hover over him and tell him all the ways he was doing it wrong. In the end, he started to feel incapable of caring for his own child, which made the experience miserable for him.

Nobody likes unsolicited advice. If I feel compelled to give advice when it hasn't been asked for, I often use the measure, "Is it going to matter in 10 years?" (Certainly, the way you put a diaper on your baby would not matter ten years later.) If it isn't something that will matter in a decade, I shut my mouth. If it is, I will be gentle about it. "Do you think doing it this way might work?" A gentle approach could be the saving grace if you absolutely feel the need to step in.

ENTITLEMENT

Nobody likes someone who acts entitled. Sometimes this behavior will show up in subtle ways. If you expect that a man will pay, open doors, and pull out chairs for you, that's all fine and good. You're old-fashioned and most men like doing these things, going back to igniting that masculine energy where he wants to protect you and keep you safe. But don't be obnoxious about it. If you both run to the car and he doesn't open the door for you, don't get in a huff or act dejected. Just be cool – men don't *have* to do those things.

When a woman acts so entitled that she forgets her manners, it's a huge red flag. He will be thinking, what is life going to be like with this woman? So even when he takes the time to open a door for you or pay for dinner, be sure to remember to say thank you. A please and thank you go a long way. These courtesies should be a lifelong thing that you carry with you, and that includes being courteous of your partner, from day one to when you're old and grey together. A solid relationship is built on honesty, trust, love, and being courteous should not wane as your relationship grows.

Now that you have a few great tips on how to avoid turning off the man of your dreams, it's time to page over to Section 11: *Using Words to Your Advantage.* This section will focus on what to say and how to say it.

USING WORDS TO YOUR ADVANTAGE

I want to focus this chapter on voluptuous vocabulary. Sometimes someone can say something to you that has a deep and meaningful impact or that never leaves you. Sometimes this statement isn't life-changing, but it can change how you see someone or feel about them and yourself. What you say to the right man can make all the difference to how they want to commit to you. Sometimes it's not what you say, but how you say it.

Remember when speaking to him in person to use an upbeat and pleasant tone. I have found that tone is very important when it comes to dating. I have a friend, her name is Kristy, and she was always the star of the show if we were out. Men would gravitate to her like moths to a flame. It was frustrating. I focused more on being down to earth, and to be honest; I was probably a little dull in comparison to her. But when I figured out what her secret was, I started to use it myself, and bam! It worked. Men loved talking to me.

What did I do? I changed my tone and the *type* of words I used. I adopted an upbeat tone when talking to men. I wasn't *excitable,* but I kind of was, if you know what I mean. I got a bit more animated, and I started using *positive* words. That probably sounds a little strange. What are positive words? Most people don't know this, but they use negative words.

Take a simple sentence as an example: "Not only does this product clean and shine your car, but it makes it fresh-smelling too." That's not a negative message, but it starts with a negative word. "not."

Spend a few days paying attention to how you word things. Are there ways you can use more positive language? Start practicing that habit today!

SENSUALITY

Grabbing a man's attention and keeping it can be a lot easier than you think if you know what to say. I have found that sensuality is important in keeping a man fixated on you. You're getting to know a guy, and you're starting to have a few dates or hang out – not is the time to unleash your sensuality in what you say.

Sometimes you have to kind of 'get into it.' The quickest way to get into the act is to imagine yourself sensually eating a juicy strawberry.

Warning: the following tips may land you in bed!

Before we begin, you must establish trust. Obviously, this advice is not for the first date, although you can tease a little with variations on this material if you're brave.

Don't say anything you aren't super comfortable saying, or it will come out sounding awkward – this happened to me once, so learn from my mistakes rather than your own!

If you're going to attempt this, a few things to remember about your speech: tap into that feminine tone of voice, speak slowly, don't rush, and get into it with your whole body.

Here are a few things to get you started:

- **Compliment him.** "I love the way you look in those jeans," or "I can't get enough of how you smell." Get your body into it, like you can't resist him. The right guys go wild for this stuff.
- **Recall the last time you were together.** "I love the way you did _____ the last time we were together," or communicate something that turned you on. Men love to know when they did well, and your lovemaking will be so much better if you share what makes you feel good. Practice makes perfect! It doesn't have to be sexual, by the way.
- **When hanky-panky happens, it's fun to be enthusiastic.** Being a little louder, making noises that tell him he's hitting all the right spots, guiding his hands, and lots of non-verbal communication are as all amazing for him as they are for you. Since we're talking about verbal communication here, don't be shy in telling him, "Harder!" "Don't stop!" or saying his name. Playing the role of being assertive, or letting him dominate you, can be fun. Most men love when we initiate things because they fear rejection, just like we do. Taking the reins for a night can turn into a very hot night for both of you.

Alternately, letting him "do whatever he wants" can also be a zesty adventure. If you've already established trust, allowing him to lead the way as you go with the flow can make for a memorable night.

- **Tips for Talking & Connecting**. Perhaps you're not at the stage where sensual talk can make an appearance in your relationship. Maybe you're just getting out there and meeting new men, in which case, you still need to know what to say, and you probably don't want to use bedroom talk. Here are a few talking points that will help you grab a guy's attention and have him wanting to talk to you all night long! He will want your number, and he will keep coming back for more.

- **Make things fun.** Before I met my partner, I would spend time in bars socializing. I also attended more backyard barbecues than I can remember. I was getting out there, and there were men for the picking. But there were a lot of women too. I found that when women sit around and *expect* men to do the talking and come and "win them over," men tend to lose interest. In those scenarios, that's when you find men huddled around the barbecue glugging beer or leaning on the bar slugging back shots with each other and not the women. I learned that making things fun made men want to talk to me more. Hearing about someone's day is a bit bland, but if you meet a girl who ching-chong-chas to see who if you or she will buy the next drink, that's fun. A girl who tells a joke or asks how *he* is doing is enticing. A girl who heads to the bar to order you her signature cocktail and teaches you a quirky cheers rhyme is *fun*. Don't be scared to tell fun stories about when you were a kid or something hilarious you saw at work yesterday are all far more enticing than the usual boring conversations that go around.

- **Be positive.** When talking to men, keep it positive. If you're droning on about the floods in a foreign country or moaning about the cost of your latest car service, the chances are you'll come across as a bit of a killjoy. Speak about positive things. Before I went out and about, I would arm myself with positive news and information. It's not weird hopping on Google to find some fun and positive things to talk about when you're socializing, and I strongly recommend it.

- **Ask about *his* life.** I will never forget this party I went to a few years ago. I met a cute guy who was upbeat, charismatic, and witty – that's my type by the way! I wanted to talk to him, and he was very interested in talking to me. So I took the plunge, walked over, and started chatting. One of the first questions I asked him was, "What are your parent's names?" He gave me a quizzical look, and he said, "Do you always ask strangers about their parents?" We both laughed, and he went on to tell me about his dad, who was his role model. From the moment I asked that unusual question about his life, he was hooked instead of focusing on me and what he should be doing to get my attention. He wanted to talk to me all night. *Some interesting questions to ask someone when you want to get to know about their life (these are fun and get a guy interested).*

- Do you have any pets?

- What did you have for breakfast? (this always gets a guy smiling for some reason)

- What does your morning wake-up alarm sound like?
- What's that one movie you loved as a kid but ruined it for yourself by watching it as an adult?
- What's your hangover strategy?
- What is the weirdest thing you've ever eaten?

These are just some examples. I recommend coming up with your own list and switch them up. You won't regret it!

Hopefully, this chapter has got you thinking a little deeper about the way you communicate with the men around you. What you say and how you say it really can make all the difference.

With that, it's time to move onto the next section. Page over to Section 12: *Positively Positive Associations*. This with how you can create positive associations to keep a man coming back for more.

POSITIVELY POSITIVE ASSOCIATIONS

Here's the thing, men like to do the things that they enjoy. Men also like to spend time with people that make them feel good. There's a very true saying that I would like you to remember: "It's not what you say to a person, it's how you make them feel."

Consider how he feels when he's with you. Do you make him feel good about himself? Does he open up to you? What does he say when you're together? Does he smile at you, make lots of eye contact, and reach for your hand? Making a man feel good whenever he is with you is a good way to help him form a positive association with spending time with you. Positive associations are what have people coming back for more. Remember that pizza place you had *the best* night at with your friends a few months back? You want to go back there just because it was so much fun, right? It works the same with people!

If you plan evenings that end in fights and misery, the chances are that he will resort to developing a negative association to doing those things with you, and you will miss out on your chance of being with Mr. Right.

It works the same in reverse, though. The more good times a guy has with you, the more time he will want to spend with you. So, make every experience a pleasant one for him. Here's the thing about positive associations: you can use it on a guy you like and often see out, or you can use it on a group of guys if you want to get them all interested in you. It works.

You can use a very effective psychological trick to help you create a sense of positive association. What is it? It's making it all about them. Of course, you don't have to be a doormat, but you should make it seem like the time you are spending with them or the attention you are giving him is all about him. You want to make eye contact, laugh at his jokes, compliment him, sneak a smile at him, ask him about his life, find out his favorite things. Just keep bringing it back to him. That's step one. Step two is being elusive. You don't want to lay it all out there for him. Once you've got his attention and he feels like he is the only guy in the room, move away and go talk to your girlfriends. This activates his chase instinct. If you've carried out step one correctly, he should come over to you or, at the very least, keeping looking in your direction to see when you will be free. Do this every time you are with a guy. Give him your undivided attention, make it fun, and then create just a little bit of distance to allow him to watch you have fun or enjoy a conversation.

You can take this positive associations trick to the next level when you're starting to get to know a guy. First, find out what his favorite things are. This includes his favorite bands (and specific songs), foods, bars/restaurants, pastimes, and color. Next time you suggest a meetup, offer to pick him up. Have his favorite music playing in the car. Head to his favorite bar for drinks and a nice touch, be wearing his favorite color. See what I did there? You have now created a situation where all of his favorite things are in one place – this is a memory he will hang onto without even thinking about it. Don't be obvious, though. Don't tell him you specifically bought a CD with his top pick of songs or that you specifically chose your dress because it's his favorite color. That will break the magic spell of positive associations.

By creating favorable situations, aka "good memories", you will build a highly positive association in your man's mind, and that's something that keeps relationships strong and men committed.

Positive associations lay the groundwork for what's called "the relationship high."

"This is the happy stage (the "relationship high") where we cannot bear to be away from the other person. It is here that you might plan all of your free time together and begin to create a private relational culture. Going out to parties and socializing with friends takes a back seat to more private activities such as cooking dinner together at home or taking long walks on the beach. Self-disclosure continues to increase as each person has a strong desire to know and understand the other. In this stage, we tend to idealize one another in that we downplay faults (or don't see them at all), seeing only the positive qualities of the other person."

This is part of normal, healthy relationship building, and it doesn't last forever, as the term "high" hints at. These awesome beginnings create those love goggles where you can't see anything wrong with the other person, and it's an important part of the finding-a-man process.

Creating these positive associations should be sincere and heartfelt, not forced. Don't be doing all this work to get his favorite meal or beer or music if you aren't that serious about him. That's just playing with his heart, and it's not cool.

If you truly feel he's the one for you, you will find that both of you are trying your best to make the other happy. As I said before, though, none of us is responsible for anyone else's happiness, so unless this effort is coming straight from your heart, don't do it just to see how far you can get into this guy's heart. Don't be the girl who is in love with the idea of being in love - she's only going to settle. And we don't settle, ladies!

SYNCHING WITH A NEW LOVE INTEREST (EMOTIONAL COORDINATION)

Moving forward, assume that he is the guy for you and you're serious about building a relationship with him, and he seems to feel the same way. You will find that the two of you will become pretty synced when it comes to certain things if you're working on it. This may be clumsy and awkward at first, but that's part of the fun. Men tend to feel emotionally positive when a couple is in full cooperation. Doing things together, such as making dinner or participating in an activity together (think of a picnic, a hike, an adventure), can invoke positive feelings for a man.

Let's say you are building a piece of furniture together or driving to a destination you've never been to, and you find him slow to act, or worse, forging ahead without reading the instructions/map. You might feel frustrated and want to snap at him. Don't. Learn self-control.

Whether we like it or not, our attitude can change the attitude of the person with us. Men tend to show a negative emotional response if the woman is feeling negative emotions. This emotional coordination is a normal human response, so if you're finding yourself growing impatient with a situation, remember to take a breath and regroup.

I like this little bit of information, and perhaps you will like it too: "...empathy can include a conscious aspect often referred to as perspective-taking, whereby partners purposefully try to understand each other's emotions better. Evidence that this could impact emotional coordination comes from a study in which greater interpersonal sensitivity was associated with more emotional coordination (Schöebi, 2008)."

What's funny is, if this furniture building or mysterious adventure isn't working out, you both might find yourself in a negative emotional state and commiserate about it! Having these life moments to laugh at together leads to bonding and funny memories to reflect on down the road. Take a breath when you want to snap, and remember that all you will do is create a negative association, which can kill a relationship.

According to a study by Larson and Almeida in 1999, "Emotional coordination can also come about, however, when partners disagree with one another, causing shared negative emotions. Therefore, various interpersonal dynamics can produce emotional coordination for both positive and negative emotions."

Relationships take effort. That effort comes in a million ways, but the big ones include communication, respect, and positive associations. Never forget that.

Spend some time thinking about how you can create positive associations with the men you meet. It's a powerful tool, so be careful how you use it and who you use it on! Ready to take things to the next level? Let's page over to Section 13: *Financial Independence is hot!*

FINANCIAL INDEPENDENCE IS HOT!

Guess what, ladies! Emotionally needy girls are not hot, and neither are financially needy girls! It's a huge turn-off for men. If spending time with you leaves a man clutching his wallet, the chances are that you're doing it all wrong.

I have a friend; for the sake of privacy, let's call her Sue. Sue would often come out with our group of friends and spend the entire night sidling up to the guys to get drinks, snacks, and whatever else was going. When the bill came around, Sue was nowhere to be seen, or she would sit there with an entitled look on her face, not even doing the obligatory scratch around in her purse to make it look like she intended to pay. Of course, nobody ever commented to Sue about it, but once when we were out, and Sue wasn't there, I heard one of the guys make a joke about it and saying that it was better she wasn't there because then they would have to pay for her fun begrudgingly. Nobody likes a user, and even if you think people don't notice, they do.

Men love an independent woman, especially women who are financially independent. And it has nothing to do with men being cheapskates. They want to provide and spoil, but they don't want it to be *expected* of them. You know, the whole theory of someone getting a thrill from doing something on their own accord, whereas if you force it or expect it, the magic is kind of sucked out of the situation.

For decades, society has placed an incredible amount of pressure on men to be the providers in a relationship. While that is the role some men choose to play, others have worked hard by going to school, landing their dream job, or starting a business that, quite frankly, they may not be ready to share with others, even a hot woman! Sure, paying for dinner here and there might be their love language, but nobody wants to be taken advantage of.

Dating a financially independent woman eases some of the pressure, and lowering that stress could positively benefit him. I can't speak for all men, obviously, but a reasonable person, man, or woman, understands that if you want to build a life together, it's going to take money. Do you want to get married, buy a house, have kids? Congratulations, it all requires money. You can't be a Pollyanna and say, "Love is enough," because, let's face it, it isn't. If you're going to cultivate any relationship, you will have to pull your weight.

If you go on a date with a guy, and you don't at least offer to pay your share, you weren't raised right. Arguably, if he doesn't pay for the entire date, he is deemed 'not raised right.' Choose what kind of woman you want to be; a gracious receiver or someone who demands and expects obnoxiously?

Making the offer matters. Why? Because after the 3rd or 4th date, you should totally say "This one is on me" and pay. Are you surprised, especially after everything I said about masculine and feminine energy? You shouldn't be.

Here's the thing. Men report that they are pleasantly surprised when a woman offers to pay. This is not something a guy will bring up to a woman he is dating. It's much more likely he'll just hold on to this resentment about it and expose it later on. He might even decide to stop going on dates with this woman because he feels taken for granted.

This dating stuff is pretty surface level and may be overlooked if the man decides he can look past this kind of thing. For early days, there's no need to share your bank statements in a PowerPoint presentation!

Of course, if you get into a serious relationship, you should share information on financial matters. For instance, if you're drowning in student and credit card debt, it may affect the groceries you buy together, the kind of dates you go on, and those holidays he seems to be planning – honesty is key, but only at the *right* time. So, to have this conversation means you need to get straight with yourself first, and you need to be confident. That takes some self-work.

Life throws us all into difficult situations from time to time. Unfortunately, it doesn't always go according to plan, but if we come to our potential life partner and tell them, "Hey, this is how things are, and this is my plan," that will be more welcomed than burying it and having it all come back to haunt us later.

Nobody is perfect.

You might enter a relationship with debt or financial issues, but if you're able to confide in your partner that you're doing something about it, it's a good idea to lay it all out there. Your confidence and the perceived competence in you dealing with it become attractive in and of itself.

I only say all that because many young people just starting their lives out will relate.

Let's say you're a young professional who figured out her financial planning early. First of all, good for you! This makes you all the more appealing to a man because you ease the societal pressure on him to provide. It's more than just that. Don't assume that all independent women are power-wielding witches with control issues.

A successful woman at work may be a powerful force in the boardroom but be comfortable enough at home to be the soft sensual woman she wants to be. The characteristics of successful women don't always include bossiness, bitchiness, or bullish stubborn qualities. A mature and secure man will appreciate a successful woman and not be intimidated by a woman who has dominated the hierarchy in the office and/or out earns him every year.

That same mature, secure man may really enjoy the fact that he doesn't have to kill himself with 70-hour work weeks to make the life that the two of you are capable of making together. Many men truly enjoy the teamwork associated with being a part of a couple, at least until you decide together that you want things to change, as in having kids or whatever you two decide your future holds.

The other thing about being a financially independent woman in a relationship is that you've already established you know the value of money. You're not going to be spending his money exorbitantly on everything you desire. You're the type who is thinking ahead. Being financially literate at a young age can set you up for a lot less unnecessary hardship down the road. (Honestly, why don't they teach this stuff in schools? When is the last time you used quadratic equations? A course on the stock market or retirement plans would have given us all so much more prepared for life!

FINANCIAL INDEPENDENCE SHOULD BE PART OF WHO YOU ARE

Financial independence is like any other personality trait. It makes up a part of who you are. However, financial independence has varying levels of importance depending on the individual and the relationship. Would you rather be the girl that heads to a bar and knows that she can afford to get herself there and back as well as pay her way, or do you want to take your chances accepting paid-for drinks from strangers – make wise choices, ladies!

Women and men must both be independent in this day and age, but especially women. Higher divorce rates, the loss of a spouse, lack of pension, and no one to look after you can be devastating, even without the financial setbacks.

Men respect independent women who take pride in their careers and have a good handle on their money. Things can get sticky when you take things too far, such as complaining too much about spending money, because he may not want to think about it or be held back from doing something fun like buying concert tickets or a vacation. Understandably, it's important to have that open communication about all subjects. Money is one of the topics that couples most often fight about, so the two of you need to be able to talk about it freely from the beginning.

The most important thing in the relationship is mutual respect for both parties, no matter the salary levels or who the breadwinner is, male or female. Just because one party is a manager or a high-level executive at work doesn't mean they get to treat their partner the same way they treat their staff, or worse, belittling them or controlling the cash flow.

We've all heard of too many stories where a woman is stuck in a situation because she cannot feasibly get herself out of a relationship due to lack of money. Don't let yourself be that girl. You want new love prospects to see you are financially independent and then feel confident that you're paying them attention because you're genuinely interested in *him*, not his wallet or paycheck.

FINANCES LATER ON IN A RELATIONSHIP

During the early stages of a relationship, both partners may be more financially equal, but once they get married and have children, one partner may decide to stay at home or work less or take a less stressful job. Everyone contributes to the relationship differently, and it is important for each individual to feel respected and have equal power. Any wife would hate getting her husband's approval to buy something, whether she was working or not. It's not acceptable. At the same time, it's key to consider your partner and family when making purchases and how they will be affected. You wouldn't go out and buy a new car and leave nothing in the account to cover the mortgage or groceries. It's important to talk about things and respect each other's decisions. Mutual respect is just as sexy as financial independence.

TOP 10 MONEY-SAVING TIPS FOR SINGLE GIRLS

Of course, this isn't a finance book, and it's not a money lesson either, but it will help your dating life a *lot* if you have a few money-saving tips up your sleeve, so you don't squander your future savings.

Here are a few tips that helped me:

- **Go over your budget (list of expenses) and eliminate unnecessary expenses** (magazine subscriptions, mobile apps, etc.)
- **Use a money rounding app to boost your savings.** When you spend $4,80, wouldn't it be great to round it up to $5 and have $0,20 to automatic savings? You get to save without even thinking about it. Forbes lists the best money rounding apps for savings – you can check them out here: https://www.forbes.com/advisor/personal-finance/the-5-best-round-up-apps-for-saving-money/
- **Stop buying take-away coffee on the go.** Get a travel mug and make your own coffee.
- **Make your own work lunches**. Stop buying food while at work or on the go – it's a massive money-waster.
- **Once you're getting to know someone** (and you're sure they're not a serial killer), **opt for dinner dates at home instead of out at a bar or restaurant.**
- **Embark on free adventures.** Not every Saturday should be sat at the bar drinking and eating your money away. Go on hikes, go play Frisbee in the park, head out for a stroll, go visit all the free tourist

attractions in your town. Your fun time doesn't have to cost you an arm and a leg.

- **Have bare-bones months where you cut back on all expenses.** Turn your heating down, suspend your streaming accounts, don't eat out – you can come up with your own bare-bones strategy.
- **Carpool when you need to go places.**
- **Use coupons and discounts**. They're not embarrassing. What's embarrassing is being offered a way to save and turning your nose up at it.
- **Negotiate contracts.** Got a mobile phone on contract? Renegotiate your rate. Do the same with your insurance and other regular contracts.

Now that you know you've got to get your finances in order to start attracting the right men, let's move on to the next section. In Section Fourteen: *Love Yourself Enough to Set Boundaries*, we address healthy boundaries and how to set them.

LOVE YOURSELF ENOUGH TO SET BOUNDARIES

All healthy relationships have a foundation built on boundaries. There are your personal boundaries, dating boundaries, co-habitation boundaries, the list goes on.

Here are some examples of boundaries for you to consider when discovering yourself before dating someone, while dating in general, and when committing to that one special person.

- **Asking permission.** This isn't about control. Asking permission to touch someone, asking permission to borrow something, basically asking permission in the context of courtesy. i.e., "Do you mind if I take the leftovers for lunch tomorrow?"
- **Consider his feelings.** This goes hand-in-hand with courtesy and can go a long way in making the other person feel valued. It's not just about anticipating their needs; it's also about when you aren't around each other. It could be something as simple as snapping up his favorite spot to sit in the

park on a date or deciding what to share with your girlfriends when the conversation turns naughty. (Hint: If you aren't sure what you can share with your girlfriends, ask yourself how you would feel about him sharing things with his guy friends. Ew.)

- **Gratitude.** We spoke about this one earlier. Simple manners and showing appreciation can go a long way. I remember my grandmother once telling my Papa that she appreciated how hard he worked for their family. He beamed with pride, and I know it meant a lot to him. Show gratitude in any number of ways: say it, show him through sweet gestures, or thank him for a great night, even if you're not dating. Keep this up, and you'll find he does the same for you!

- **Honesty.** Now this goes without saying, but BE HONEST even if you've found yourself in a pickle. Once trust is broken, it is almost always impossible to get it back. Sure, couples who have survived infidelity have made it work, but don't you think that crack in their foundation will affect them forever? Start with the little things while you're just getting to know a guy. Don't lie about your past, your reasons for doing things, why you're late, or how someone treated you. Keep your honesty in check, and it will become a natural thing as the relationship develops.

- **Avoid codependency and give people their own space – have your own lives.** The word "allowed" shouldn't be a thing in your relationship. Don't you just cringe at couples where the wife will say, "Oh yeah, Jim is *allowed* to go on that fishing trip!" Gross. Jim shouldn't need permission to spend time away from his wife at all. It's healthy to have your own lives, your own careers, hobbies, friends, activities, sports, clubs - whatever makes you feel like a whole and complete independent person!

- **Be respectful of different perspectives, viewpoints, and feelings.** This one can be tricky. You may be socializing with men and hear something you don't like and immediately jump on it aggressively. That's not going to do much for your attractiveness levels. Treat people with respect even if you disagree with them. Many couples in the world do not see eye to eye in political or religious contexts. You know what? They don't have to! Respecting each other's choices on who to vote for, or what church to go to (if at all), should be an acceptable thing. You can have a perfectly healthy relationship where one spouse enjoys his Sunday morning at the local church, and his wife decides that isn't for her. You can vote differently. Now there may be some things you don't see eye to eye on that become dealbreakers, and hopefully, you discover them early on. Certain things can be real turn-offs that make the relationship dead in the water, such as drug use, smoking, racism, or sexism. You can still be respectful and say goodbye in those cases! But generally speaking, being respectful of different perspectives and viewpoints can bring your relationship to new levels where you both learn something. And being respectful of each other's feelings should just be a given. If you hurt him with your words, you need to respect how he feels at that moment. Put yourself in his shoes. You don't get to tell anyone how they should feel, especially if you're the one who made them feel that way.

- **Be aware of his emotional communication.** This ties in with the last one, of course. Be cognizant of how he's telling you when he's upset, and hopefully, he will get to know your style as well. When you're just starting to date guys, that first upset or squabble will eventually come along, and how you handle it is quite important. Some people need to cool down before they discuss a conflict. Some people need to talk things out. Some people want to ignore the situation completely and move on, which isn't ideal. Learning to figure out where he's at while facing conflict is something you need to work on. Furthermore, using "I feel" statements when communicating in conflict can be beneficial to both parties to recognize when feelings have been hurt.

- **Accountability.** This is simple. If you messed up, admit it. He should do the same. If you're dating anyone with integrity, this should be an easy one. If he has trouble taking accountability and is consistently blaming others, this is a red flag.

RED FLAGS OFTEN DISGUISED AS BOUNDARIES

Do not confuse boundaries with trying to gain control of yourself. If he's put forth any of these boundaries, know this: he is not a good guy. Say goodbye!

- Telling you how to dress
- Expecting to have a say in how do you everything (see friends, cut your hair)
- Giving you ultimatums
- Repeated attempts to "test" you or trick you, i.e., creating a fake profile to trap you into cheating
- Threatening to harm himself because you won't comply with his demands

- Giving you timelines as to when to be in his presence
- Reaction formation (showing an opposite emotion of what is felt)
- Lying
- Split personalities – fine one day, raging the next. When you never know what you're going to get, it's unnerving and often escalates to an unsafe situation.
- Engaging in behaviors that make you second guess yourself (gaslighting)
- Stonewalling – shutting down during conflict, giving the silent treatment, sometimes for days on end.
- Attempting to isolate you from your friends and family
- Little regard for your health and safety – i.e., risky behavior, asking you to stick by them during a confrontation with someone else
- Domestic violence or sexual violence

The bottom line here is that if your gut instinct is telling you that something is off about this person, trust your gut. Some people are so good at manipulating people; you don't even notice it's happening, or you end up making excuses for him because the relationship is new, and you have those love goggles on. You don't want to be the frog in the pot that doesn't realize the water is getting warmer and then boils alive because it happened so gradually.

I strongly recommend that you put a bit of time and thought into what type of boundaries are healthy for you when you're getting out there meeting new men and when you eventually start dating. While you're thinking about that, let's move on to the next section: Section 15: *Killing Dead-End Relationships – 6 Simple Rules.*

KILLING DEAD-END RELATIONSHIPS – 6 SIMPLE RULES

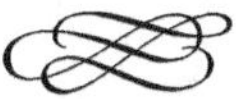

Most of us have been *there* – in dead-end relationship territory. It may be that there's "nothing wrong" with the relationship, but it's really going nowhere. This section covers why killing dead-end relationships are important, how to avoid them, and how to go about working up to ending them if you end up in them.

KNOW YOURSELF & WHAT YOU WANT

Would you consider yourself desperate? Are you tired of being single? Are you looking for some physical activity in the sheets? Make sure you know who you are and your dating goals before you get into a relationship. You're likely setting yourself up for a dead-end relationship if you're looking for temporary love or filling a void.

Ask yourself a few important questions. Why are you in the dating world in the first place? Which qualities are you looking for in a guy? What makes a man appealing to you? When dating without knowing your goals, wants, and needs, you may inadvertently end up in a dead-end relationship, despite all of your best intentions. Determine what your real dating goals are, and make sure you have them in mind.

Being prepared and ready for a relationship is an important part of making it work. If you're not at a point in your life where you can juggle work/school and a relationship, you might want to re-evaluate when would be a good time to begin dating. Involving yourself in a relationship while you are already busy will more than likely result in wasted time and a dead-end relationship.

Play the field! You don't have to date one guy at a time; in fact, you probably shouldn't. My own grandmother used to tell me to play the field and get to know what I like and what I don't!

Keeping it fresh by dating many different people is one of the keys to avoiding a dead-end relationship. Don't just date men who fit your ideal list; date guys who are a little out of the ordinary, too. It will help you eliminate any relationships with people you're not interested in and narrow down what type of guy you're looking for. You may be surprised what appeals to you once you get into the dating pool and go from paddling in the shallow end to synchronized swimming. Go out in groups of friends, try some new things, be carefree, and enjoy yourself!

RESPECT YOURSELF

Relationships with no future are pointless. Spending your time on someone and a relationship that is doomed from the start is one of the last things you want to do. Remember that your time is precious if you want to avoid these types of relationships. There's no need to waste time on something that won't work, nor should you want to. Spend your precious time on people you trust and enjoy.

In respecting yourself, avoid men who are unavailable in every sense. It will almost always end in failure. There's no point in dating a married man since it will only be a short fling. A man who is emotionally closed up and walled off won't bring you anything good either. Look for a person who is accessible on an emotional, physical, and mental level.

DON'T DATE UNDER PRESSURE

Do your friends pressure you to date this man? When people find out you've been single for so long, do they poke fun at you? Is your mom on your case to date her trainer, her dentist, and the boy at the tennis club? Are you tired of being single? It is unlikely that you will have a successful relationship if you date someone out of desperation or due to pressure. You should date a man because you want to and not because you feel pressured into doing so. Certainly, don't succumb to pressure from anyone, but especially not from a man that is pressuring you to date him.

GET TO KNOW HIM

To commit to a relationship with a guy, it is important to get to know him completely. Make sure you know him inside and out before getting into a relationship with him. Being blindly involved in a relationship can result in all types of problems, as well as a dead-end relationship. Being in a relationship with someone without really knowing him can be challenging.

Get to know each other on a deeper level before jumping ahead to the next steps. Any relationship must have a solid foundation if it is going to last. If you are dating each other only because the action between the sheets is good, don't expect the relationship to last. Make sure that you can connect on a deeper level with your partner to avoid a dead-end relationship. A relationship can't be sustained and strengthened based on physical attraction alone.

YOU DON'T HAVE TO CONTINUE A FLING IF IT'S NOT GONNA BE A THING!

It is okay to cut a man off if you are not "feeling it" with him or you're noticing many red flags. There is nothing wrong with telling a man "no," even if he wines and dines you as part of an attempt to become something more. Saying no will keep you out of trouble and keep you from wasting time and energy.

Knowing the signs is important. If you are in a dead-end relationship, you will notice a few obvious signs. These signs are useful to recognize in order to avoid them in the future. You might feel bored, or you might feel like you are settling. Lack of chemistry or poor communication are indications. If you feel that things are stagnant, or you find yourself avoiding him but can't articulate why it's time to explore these feelings and discover what's keeping you from taking your relationship further. Clearly, it's dead-end if you feel negative about a relationship and don't see it going anywhere.

Don't ignore red flags! Some relationships are bound to have a red flag or two, but when these red flags start racking up into the double digits, it's time to bail. Keep a mental tab of the number of red flags that this man has set off, and how those things make you feel. If he acts really sketchy and entirely uninterested, you may be destined for a dead-end relationship.

Some red flags can be ignored and forgiven; others are a true sign of warning, like the ones we discussed earlier.

FAIL GRACEFULLY

Make sure you learn from any dead-end relationships you may have had in the past. Your past relationships and dating history need not repeat themselves. Don't hesitate to break things off as quickly as possible if this new relationship feels like a bad experience that you've had before. It's best for both of you.

Don't settle. You are a queen, and you deserve the best guy for *you*! It doesn't matter whether you're unhappy, he's unhappy, or both of you are unhappy. No one should settle just because they feel it's their only option. There is also an obvious problem when you settle with a guy that's not entirely right for you. You won't be able to fulfill your needs for very long if you get into a relationship because you are lonely or because you want someone to romance you.

In most cases, settling leads to a strained or dead-end relationship. You're going to know you settled, and he's never going to be good enough for you. He will never meet your needs and standards. You did all this work to become the amazing person that you are. Respect yourself to choose a partner that matches your efforts and makes you feel amazing.

Now, that you have all the equipment you need to avoid dead-end relationships, let's move on to the next section. Section 16: *Be More Than the Woman He Fell In Love With* provides helpful tips on self-growth and how you can become an even better woman for a man after he has fallen in love with you. Page over to the next section.

BE MORE THAN THE WOMAN HE FELL IN LOVE WITH

Here's the thing, we all change and grow over time. And if this guy has fallen in love with you, he will change and grow too. You are both going to be more than the person you each fell in love with. You will improve within yourselves and help each other be the best version of yourselves. A supportive relationship allows the participants to grow in all facets of life, such as career, personality, finance, and between each other if you know what I mean!

As you mature together, you will run into situations where you need to work as a team to solve things or change things. It's going to be that initial foundation that you built that will carry you through those tough times. If your relationship is built on trust, respect, and collaboration, the two of you will weather storms that you don't even know are on the horizon.

Life is going to throw some crazy challenges at you: perhaps the loss of a pregnancy or child, sickness, job loss, and a whole host of other day-to-day occurrences that are unexpected. But, life is also going to bring you great joy: your first home, maybe kids or dogs or cats, promotions, successes, or perhaps a lottery win. In these ups and downs, you want to be with someone who will hug you when you're sad, listen when you need an ear, and playfully punch you in the arm to encourage you to help do a chore. You're going to want a teammate in each other, someone you can count on. Be that person for him, and trust me, he will be that person for you too. Treat him how you want to be treated, and you will be rewarded with a lifelong, great love fit for the storybooks.

Being more than the woman he fell in love with usually happens naturally. If you were the type of girl who took the time to get to know herself and what she wanted, and you set your course as best you could, you will end up with the guy that shares similar goals and life plans with you. He will be the one you choose because you saw things in him like integrity, kindness, and respect.

Being more than the man you fell in love with will also be organic for him. He will try harder at work, try to be the best boyfriend in the world, and if he feels safe and secure with you by his side, he's going to do these things joyfully and with enthusiasm.

Here are a few tips on being more than the woman he fell in love with:

KEEP YOUR COOL AND STAY EASY-GOING

Remain open to change because life plans can get derailed in both positive and negative ways. A promotion could result in an unplanned move across the country. A sick relative might change employment as one of you has to care for them. A serious illness may throw your whole life off course, so you want to have a relationship in which both of you feel stable and secure in that you can trust each other to handle whatever comes your way. A key component of a healthy relationship is knowing you can count on each other.

AVOID COMPLACENCY

I've discussed complacency a few times in this book. It's easy to 'let yourself go,' especially when you've had a couple of kids, and you just want a glass of wine and a nap on a random Tuesday. If you get to the parenting and marriage part – which I know you will – know that these things are not easy.

I once read an article in a magazine written by a woman accusing the average married woman of "False Advertising." The author explained that when you were dating, you made a concerted effort to look and smell nice, you wore lingerie and were passionate and adventurous in bed, you kept a clean house, and you had your life together. Fast forward 3-5 years into marriage, post-kids: you're frazzled, trying to hold together your career and home life in a delicate balance, your kids demand all your energy, and your sexy heels have been shoved to the back of a closet and haven't seen the light of day in some time. The last time you had "relations" was sometime last summer, and you shave your legs with the cycles of the moon. The author's premise was that this was why 50% of marriages end in divorce. Because of us women. Disappointing failures, all of us!

As you can well imagine, women everywhere were pretty offended by the article. Moms wrote in to defend their lack of time and energy and were quick to blame their spouses because 'If only they had a little help,' things would be different.

The role of women has changed drastically since the 1950s. Because women are responsible for so much more than they were 70 years ago, men have embraced new roles and responsibilities. Where before they were hands-off with parenting or household chores, nowadays they are generally all in.

This enormous societal shift has not always been fair to men and women as we all try to navigate these roles. The best relationships involve teamwork and compromise, and the relationships that thrive do so because both parties put in as much effort as possible.

While the author of the 'False Advertising' article might have missed the mark in some ways, she made good points about continuing efforts to seduce each other, respect each other, and continue to make safe spaces for each other to thrive and grow as a family.

KEEP YOUR SEX LIFE ALIVE

This section is more for couples who have been together a while and have had kids. Motherhood changes your sexuality significantly. There are many books on the subject. Regaining your sexuality after a baby is a slow, arduous process, and it can be very scary for some women. There's also a world of body image struggles that happen during and after pregnancy, and it's not even just about her body. Feeling torn between the woman she used to be and this new character called Mom, most women feel misplaced and 'not herself.' All of this is normal! Having a patient and kind partner is critical, while you navigate the messy, milky, often painful parts of new motherhood. This is where the man you committed to can shine. If he's more than the guy you fell in love with, he will step up and help, reassure you as you struggle with all the changes you are going through, and get you the help you need if it's well beyond his scope, like if you're experiencing postpartum depression. Be gentle with each other in this time and during all challenging times.

Considering each other's *feelings* through this time is more difficult, too, because you're both exhausted from the demands of a new baby in your home that disrupts your regular sleep schedules. You're both new at some of this so take a deep breath before you decide to criticize how you are handling tasks. Being tired makes most people pretty irritable, so it's easy to lose your patience with each other. It's going to be a true test of endurance in all the ways you think.

DON'T LET ROMANCE AND FUN TAKE A PLUNGE, EVEN IF YOU DON'T HAVE KIDS!

Even if you decide kids aren't for you, life can get in the way of romance so easily. Job demands, family, and friends can all affect how much energy you have for each other at the end of a week. It's important to make time for each other. Schedule it, stick to it, and make it a frequent and regular commitment to each other. It doesn't have to be expensive dinners or lavish trips. It can be any number of things that the two of you enjoy: playing on a baseball team together, camping, playing cards, or going to the Saturday morning farmer's market are all fun activities too, and they don't break the bank. Heck, even planning retirement or having a contest to see who can save the most money or unload the dishwasher faster can be fun. Embrace your inner child and be playful!

Life doesn't have to be so serious, and it's a short amount of time. You don't want to look back on your life and realize that you didn't tick at least some of the most interesting things off your bucket list. Don't hold each other back!

If you have committed to each other, you're going to look back years from now and have all kinds of inside jokes and fun moments you've shared. Recalling all the fun you've had, and all the funny moments you've experienced, you will see that it came naturally as you built your life together. Don't be those people that get so comfortable that they will say horrible nasty things to each other. Don't take your love for granted because you can lose it in the blink of an eye.

Being more than the woman he fell in love with is about choosing to be more as a person. It's going the extra mile for each other even after the excitement of the butterflies in your stomach has worn off. Continue to be an open-minded, easy-going human, and you'll be well on your way to creating a life that both of you can develop together with (mostly) peace and harmony.

Keep this in mind as you're getting to know someone. *"Is he the kind of guy you can see yourself going the extra mile for, for the rest of your life?"* While you're thinking about that, let's page over the next section, *Section 17: Let's Get Textual.*

LET'S GET TEXTUAL

The trick to texting him is to lure him in, hook, line and sinker! Men have great imaginations, and you can really play into that if you learn to have a way with words. Getting textual is a great part of bonding when getting to know a guy. It's an area I shine in! If you are talking via text, try being more descriptive than simply being direct. Give your new man something interesting to visualize and think about – boring messages don't position you as a catch!

If you have something interesting or fun to say, men will remember it. If you are merely relaying boring conversation and information, the chances are that he will forget the conversation and may even stop responding (yikes).

Of course, you want to be remembered. You want this man to think about you when he laughs about similar things in the future, even when you are not around – there's power in that. He will keep coming back for more if you give him something to remember you by.

So, what you say can have a rather profound result. Think of saying things like "I love your sense of humor" or "I really could use your advice," "You are the best storyteller I have ever met." Obviously, make your phrases relevant to your situation and the person. Everyone likes a good ego stroke, but a genuine compliment and admiration go way further than shallow ego-stroking!

When texting turns spicy, it kind of requires your full attention. Again, be descriptive. Saying things like "I want you so bad right now," and "All I can think about is your [descriptive body part]." Tell him what you want him to do to you. This is especially hot if you're away on business or out with the girls, and you talk about what you're going to do to him the next time you see him.

Men really enjoy being on the receiving end of these messages, so if you've got that trust, don't be shy!

Here are a few other gems to tuck away for later:

- "I wish I was in your bed right now."
- "You looked so gorgeous tonight; I couldn't stop staring at you."
- "We have so much time ahead of us."
- "You up?"
- "You're a keeper."
- "Thank you for always..."
- "I have plans." (Yup. Be busy once in a while)
- "You make me smile so much that my cheeks hurt!"
- "I really want pizza - and a cute guy to eat it with tonight (hint)"
- "I am so proud of you because..."
- "I hope your day is as nice as your butt ;-)"

- "Whenever I get a text from you, I cannot help but smile!"
- "There's a sale in my bedroom right now. Everything is 100% off!"
- "You, me, and a beer tonight – don't make plans for tomorrow!"
- "You make it impossible for me to focus on work"
- "You're really easy to talk to."

Speaking of trust, if you decide sending explicit pictures is the route you'll go, be careful. It's actually better for you to leave a little to the imagination and keep your face out of it. Men enjoy a little bit of mystery, and you never know whose hands that picture will eventually end up in (it could be a case of a stolen phone). Again, you have to trust the other person, but it doesn't hurt to play it safe in case things don't work out and he's not who you thought he was. A big warning is not to sext or send pics if you have not met in person yet. The internet is full of sharks, and you don't want to be sending stuff that could bite you later on. Play it safe!

Here are a few more texting ideas that will spark a guy's interest, especially if you're in the "are-we-dating / exclusive" phase.

- If you decide your relationship is ready for sharing explicit (but mysterious!) **photos**, show him what's waiting for him when he gets home/comes over. He will be so excited to see you, and he might even bail on the boys a bit early!
- **Share a private throwback moment.** Maybe you had some spicy times in his car. Remind him of it! He will enjoy that tidbit of passion and won't be able to stop thinking about the next time he sees you.

- **Be fun, send a joke or something funny!**
  Memes are great or anything by The Far Side.
- **Send him a link or screenshot of sexy lingerie you are thinking about purchasing.**
  He's going to have to use his imagination a little bit, but isn't that part of the fun?
- **Show him that you listen to what he says.**
  Send a message like, "Hey! Just wondering how that big meeting went at work?" or "Are things a little less stressful with work this week – I've been thinking of you!"
- **Plan some alone time.** Send him an official-looking email like "my place, naked, Friday at 8." He will definitely be there. Or if you want something more toned down, you can still send him a cute email with a "ticket" looking invitation to a sports event, or casual invite for a movie night at your place. The point is, is that you're going to some effort as opposed to just texting him about your date.
- **You don't have to be the only one sharing photos.** Ask for one! He's going to love that butterfly-feeling he gets, knowing it turns you on too.
- **Plan out a role play if that's your thing.**
  Order a costume and let him know he's got a date with someone else entirely this weekend!
- **Let him know that he's someone you can't get out of your mind,** especially if it's the morning after a fiery night. "I've got this presentation this afternoon, but all I can think about is last night."
- **Abrupt messages like this one are exciting:**
  "Just FYI, I'm not wearing any panties." Blink. Blink blink.

- **Tell him you had a dirty dream about him.** Of course, he's going to want to hear all about it!
- **Suggest a destination that you've never "been" before.** "START THE CAR!" And then tell him you'll be over soon (knowing he's free of course).

PLAYING THE TEXTING GAME

Now, ladies here's another sensitive topic. How often should you be texting a new love interest? I once knew a girl who texted a guy she liked so much that he stonewalled her in the end. He liked her but felt smothered by her messages. If he doesn't answer you back, it is not an invitation to send him a plethora of messages. Rather let it go.

If he does message you back, don't try to keep the banter going until 3 am. The chances are that he will get tired and think that you're a bit clingy. Know when to stop. Do you know when the conversation naturally dies down? Be the first one to stop texting. Let him be the last one to text. It's not a game, but it will keep him guessing and also leaves an "in" for you to pick up your phone and text him a few days later. You can try something fun like, "Sorry I didn't text you back; I was elbows deep in adulting. What are you up to today?"

Schedule a video or voice note day with yourself once you've been chatting for a while; schedule a video or voice note day (with yourself). Pop on a bit of makeup (don't go overboard) and video yourself going for a walk, saying how you were *just* thinking of him and wished he was joining you on your stroll. Short and sweet/cute is the way to go.

Don't see texting as a simple form of communication. Get creative and have fun with it. You want him staring down at his phone, smiling from ear to ear when he gets a message from you, not scanning the preview and leaving it "for later." Use the above messaging tactics, and you will have him coming back for more (and more and more!)

CONCLUSION

You've made it! You've covered all the essential aspects of not just getting a guy's attention but being the type of girl that keeps it. The tips and pointers might seem simple, but that's the thing. Getting a man's attention and keeping it is a lot simpler than you think it is. Men don't need extravagance and a big showy encounter to get their attention.

You will find that most men want a down-to-earth girl with who they can connect. They don't want to feel subservient and need to be at your beck and call. They want to feel respected, wanted, and needed, but more than that, they want a girl who can make them laugh and who they can laugh with. They want a woman who can handle herself at a party, work, in front of his parents, and even when another woman throws herself at him. He wants a woman who can handle that he has a life outside of the relationship and gives him the space to be who he truly is. When you make a man feel like he can be himself and always has a place with you, he will come home to you forever because you *are home*.

Take the complicated schemes and strategies you have had in your mind and ditch them. Work on becoming the type of woman who would be interesting to get to know. Develop hobbies, find passions and interests, become a well-rounded and wholesome person who enjoys life and wants to live it. When you start working on yourself and pair your new depth with a few of the conversational and behavior tactics taught in this book, you become the woman *every* man wants to be with – and that means that Mr. Right will want to be with you too.

Armed with all this information, I encourage you to create your own get-the-guy strategy that fits in with your life and your relationship desires. Finding the right man isn't something that happens by chance; it takes intentional self-growth.

Good luck!

Oh, before you go, if you liked what you read and learned in this book, please leave a positive Amazon review – I would really appreciate it.

RESOURCES

7 Sweet & Simple Secrets for Making Your Man Feel Loved. (2019, June 5). MeetMindful | A Fuller Life Together. https://www.meetmindful.com/making-your-man-feel-loved/

8 Reasons Why You Need at Least 8 Hugs a Day. (n.d.). Happify.Com. Retrieved 14 August 2021, from https://www.happify.com/hd/8-reasons-why-you-need-at-least-8-hugs-a-day/#:%7E:text=When%20people%20hug%20for%2020,immune%20system%20and%20reduce%20stress

10 ways to instantly become more attractive. (n.d.). The Art of Simple. Retrieved 18 August 2021, from https://theartofsimple.net/10-ways-to-instantly-become-more-attractive/

Borbala @ Follow Your Own Rhythm. (2018, October 16). *5 Practical Ways to be More Present With Other People.* Follow Your Own Rhythm. https://www.followyourownrhythm.com/blog-1/2018/7/24/5-practical-ways-to-be-more-present-with-other-people

Brolley, B. (2021, March 22). *Surprising things guys find unattractive.* TheList.Com. https://www.thelist.com/47981/surprising-things-guys-find-unnattractive/

Cobden, D. (n.d.). *121 Clever Texts To Send To A Guy You Like (Flirty + Irresistible).* Dateworks. Retrieved 15 August 2021, from https://dateworks.ca/dating/clever-texts-to-send-to-a-guy-you-like-witty-flirty/

Cohen, J. (2020, March 28). *Why Men Like Confident Women.* Joann Cohen Matchmaking. https://www.joanncohen.com/why-men-like-confident-women/

deBara, D. (2020, July 11). *4 Ways to Find a Hobby You Love (Because It's Good for Your Life and Your Career).* The Muse. https://www.themuse.com/advice/how-to-find-a-hobby-you-love

DIXON, M. (2016, October 18). *15 Hobbies That Make You More Attractive To Guys.* The Talko. https://www.thetalko.com/15-hobbies-that-make-you-more-attractive-to-guys/

Eze, E. (2020, November 4). *10 Really Small Things Guys Find Unattractive.* The Good Men Project. https://goodmenproject.com/featured-content/10-really-small-things-guys-find-unattractive/

Flores, E. R. (2021, January 7). *Keeping Your Relationship Alive After 10, 20, 30 Years.* Redbook. https://www.redbookmag.com/love-sex/relationships/g30678535/relationship-spark-tips/

The Future of Memory: Remembering, Imagining, and the Brain. (2012, November 21). PubMed Central (PMC). https://www.ncbi.nlm.nih.gov/pmc/articles/PMC3815616/

Gordon, S. (2020, October 28). *How to Text in a Healthy Way.* Verywell Mind. https://www.verywellmind.com/understanding-the-dynamics-of-texting-in-relationships-4769077

Gulla, E. (2020, November 5). *Red flags in relationships and dating you shouldn't ignore.* Cosmopolitan. https://www.cosmopolitan.com/uk/love-sex/relationships/a33364278/red-flags-relationship/

Hagen, K. (2021, July 18). *5 Money Habits Men Look for in a Romantic Partner*. The Motley Fool. https://www.fool.com/the-ascent/banks/articles/5-money-habits-men-look-for-in-a-romantic-partner/

Hall, J. (2014, February 24). *13 Simple Ways You Can Have More Meaningful Conversations*. Forbes. https://www.forbes.com/sites/johnhall/2013/08/18/13-simple-ways-you-can-have-more-meaningful-conversations/?sh=7869e9e74fe9

He says I'm not the same woman he fell in love with, that he doesn't need me, that I don't motivate him and that I'm lazy and not ambitious. If he thinks so low of me why is he still married to me? - Quora. (n.d.). Quora. Retrieved 14 August 2021, from https://www.quora.com/He-says-Im-not-the-same-woman-he-fell-in-love-with-that-he-doesnt-need-me-that-I-dont-motivate-him-and-that-Im-lazy-and-not-ambitious-If-he-thinks-so-low-of-me-why-is-he-still-married-to-me

Hughes, P. (2017, November 29). *8 Ways to Communicate with Men*. Positive Communication Pro. https://www.drzimmerman.com/tuesdaytip/8-ways-to-communicate-with-men

Insecurities are unattractive. Do you agree with this statement? Why or why not? - Quora. (n.d.). Quora. Retrieved 14 August 2021, from https://www.quora.com/Insecurities-are-unattractive-Do-you-agree-with-this-statement-Why-or-why-not

Johnson, A. (2018, August 6). *This List of 50 Low-cost Hobbies Will Excite You*. Lifehack. https://www.lifehack.org/articles/money/this-list-50-low-cost-hobbies-will-excite-you-2.html

Johnson, E. N. (2020, June 15). *This is why you're clinging to a relationship that's dead in the water*. Medium. https://medium.

com/lady-vivra/this-is-why-youre-clinging-to-a-relationship-that-s-dead-in-the-water-60963b64e754

LovePanky, T. (2021, June 4). *How to Talk to a Guy: 34 Tips to Sweet Talk & Make Him Like You.* LovePanky - Your Guide to Better Love and Relationships. https://www.lovepanky.com/women/attracting-and-dating-men/how-to-talk-to-a-guy-you-like

MensLine Australia. (2021, July 5). *Tips for better conversations with men.* https://mensline.org.au/relationship-advice-for-men/tips-for-better-conversations-with-men/

Miller, W. (2020, February 14). *Are You Living in a Dead Relationship? - Wendy Miller.* Medium. https://wendymillermeditation.medium.com/are-you-living-in-a-dead-relationship-5330a09f7d38

Natarajan, H. (2021, May 10). *What Makes A Man Fall Deeply In Love With A Woman?* STYLECRAZE. https://www.stylecraze.com/articles/what-makes-a-man-fall-in-love/

Nawrocki, J. (2014, March 28). 30 *Tips To Become More Confident Nobody Told You Before.* Lifehack. https://www.lifehack.org/articles/communication/30-tips-become-more-confident-nobody-told-you-before.html

Pathak, S. (2021, August 6). *Love Candles By Bath & Body Works? 10 Alternative Brands That Also Make Delicious Scented Candles.* The Channel 46. https://www.thechannel46.com/health/spirituality/7-ways-to-unlock-your-mind-tap-into-your-subconscious/

Pattemore, C. (2021, June 4). *How to Set Boundaries in Your Relationships.* Psych Central. https://psychcentral.com/blog/

why-healthy-relationships-always-have-boundaries-how-to-set-boundaries-in-yours

Phippen, A. (2018, May 10). *10 unattractive things that instantly turn guys off*. Statesboro Herald. https://www.statesboroherald.com/life/hot-topics/10-unattractive-things-that-instantly-turn-guys-off/

Positivity, P. O. (2020, November 1). *10 Reasons to Use Positive Words in Your Communications with Others*. Power of Positivity: Positive Thinking & Attitude. https://www.powerofpositivity.com/positive-words-communications-with-others/#:%7E:text=When%20you%20use%20positive%20words%20in%20your%20conversation%2C%20you%20speak,as%20positive%20relations%20and%20situations

ROBBINS RESEARCHINTERNATIONAL, INC. (2020, December 17). *How to let go of insecurities in a relationship | Tony Robbins*. Tonyrobbins.Com. https://www.tonyrobbins.com/ultimate-relationship-guide/insecure-in-a-relationship/

Sawant, N. (2020, April 23). *5 men on the personality traits they cannot resist*. Femina.In. https://www.femina.in/relationships/love-sex/personality-traits-that-guys-cant-resist-30884.html

Schanfarber, J. (2020, May 12). *7 Tips for Practicing Presence in Your Relationship*. Justice Schanfarber Counselling - Relationships, Sex, Intimacy. https://www.justiceschanfarber.com/how-to-be-present-in-your-relationship/

Smith, S. (2018, November 1). *What to do if your own insecurity is ruining your relationships*. Cosmopolitan. https://www.cosmopolitan.com/uk/love-sex/relationships/a24437388/insecure-in-relationship/

Steber, C. (2019, February 17). *9 Ways To Feel More Present With Your Partner, According To Experts*. Bustle. https://www.bustle.com/p/9-ways-to-feel-more-present-with-your-partner-according-to-experts-15954342

Sunderland, R. (n.d.). *The importance of financial independence: don't rely on a man | The Spectator*. Spectator. Retrieved 22 August 2021, from https://www.spectator.co.uk/article/the-importance-of-financial-independence-don-t-rely-on-a-man

Tehini, N. (2019, June 26). *How to Awaken and Tap Into Your Feminine Energy*. Goodness. https://goodness.me/mind/363167/how-to-tap-into-feminine-energy

Watson, C. (2020, July 10). *5 Tactics You Can Use to Tap into Your Feminine*. Women on Purpose. https://www.womenonpurpose.ca/5-tactics-you-can-use-to-tap-into-your-feminine/

wattsnext Group. (2017, January 5). *4 Tips Towards Creating A Happy And Rewarding Professional Life*. https://wattsnextgroup.com/4-tips-towards-creating-a-happy-and-rewarding-professional-life-3/

wikiHow. (2019, September 6). *How to Make a Guy Feel Special*. https://www.wikihow.com/Make-a-Guy-Feel-Special